Studies in the Modern Russian Language

GENERAL EDITOR: DENNIS WARD
Professor of Russian, University of Edinburgh

6

THE FORMATION AND EXPRESSIVE USE OF DIMINUTIVES

THE FORMATION AND EXPRESSIVE USE OF DIMINUTIVES

B. V. BRATUS
University of Leningrad

PREPARED AND SUBMITTED FOR
PUBLICATION BY THE NOVOSTI PRESS AGENCY PUBLISHERS
(APN MOSCOW)

CAMBRIDGE
AT THE UNIVERSITY PRESS
1969

Published by the Syndics of the Cambridge University Press
Bentley House, 200 Euston Road, London N.W.1
American Branch: 32 East 57th Street, New York, N.Y. 10022

© Cambridge University Press 1969

Library of Congress Catalogue Card Number: 69-11023

Standard Book Number: 521 07361 8 clothbound
521 09546 8 paperback

Printed in Great Britain
at the University Printing House, Cambridge
(Brooke Crutchley, University Printer)

CONTENTS

	Preface		*page* vii
1	Introduction		1
	A	General remarks on diminutives	1
	B	The diminutive as a means of expression in Russian	2
	C	The range of use of diminutives	3
	D	The meaning of Russian diminutives and their translation into other languages	5
	E	Degrees of diminutiveness in Russian	8
	F	Tendency for the diminutive to become more widespread in modern Russian literature	10
	G	The formation of diminutives	12
2	Diminutive suffixes of nouns		13
	A	Diminutive suffixes of the first degree of expressiveness	13
		i The suffix -ка	13
		ii The suffix -ик	18
		iii The suffix -чик	21
		iv The suffix -ок/-ёк	22
		v The suffix -(е)цо/-(и)це	24
		vi The suffix -ец	26
		vii The suffixes -ёнок/-онок and -ёныш	27
		viii The suffix -ица	28
		ix The suffix -инка	28
		x The suffix -ыш	29
		xi The suffixes -ко and -ико	29
		xii The suffix -ца	30
	B	Diminutive suffixes of the second degree of expressiveness	30
		i The suffix -енька	30
		ii The suffix -онька	31
		iii The suffix -ушка/-юшка (and -ушко/-юшко)	32
		iv The suffix -уша/-юша	33

v

			page
	v	The suffix -ышко (and -ышек)	33
	vi	The suffixes -ишко and -ишка	33
	vii	The suffix -ашка	34
	viii	The suffix -онка/-ёнка	35
c		Diminutive suffixes of the third degree of expressiveness	35
	i	The suffix -очка/-ечка	36
	ii	The suffix -ичка	38
	iii	The suffix -очек/-ёчек	38
	iv	The suffixes -оночек/-ёночек and -оночка/-ёночка	39
	v	The suffix -иночка	40
	vi	The suffixes -ишечка, -ишечко and -ушечка/-юшечка	40
	vii	The suffixes -урочка and -уленька	41
3		The formation of diminutive adjectives	42
	i	The suffix -енький/-онький	43
	ii	The suffixes -ёхонький/-охонький and -ёшенький/-ошенький	45
	iii	The suffix -юсенький/-усенький	46
	iv	The suffixes -оватый/-еватый and -оватенький/-еватенький	46
4		Diminutive forms of adverbs	49
5		The question of verbal diminutives	52
6		Conclusions	55

Appendices 56
1. Alphabetical list of diminutive noun suffixes 56
2. Grammatical and phonetic notes 58
3. Lexical sets of diminutives 60
(relationships; parts of the body; dress and footwear; food and drink; animals; trees and plants; natural phenomena; the house; household objects; materials; people, nationalities, professions; time; measures; abstract nouns)

Bibliography 68

PREFACE

Radio and television, today's media of mass communication, have considerably enhanced the role of the emotional and expressive nuances of the spoken language. The primary resources in Russian for conveying such nuances are intonation and diminutives.

The present work is devoted to the formation of diminutives and in particular to their expressive function, this being one of the most important aspects of diminutives.[1] The work contains an analysis of the formal resources of diminutives and the meanings expressed by them. A suggested classification of diminutive suffixes according to the degrees of expressiveness of the diminutives formed by them is offered, the range of use of diminutive forms is defined, and a large number of examples is given both from classical and modern literature. The illustrative material adduced allows one to draw the preliminary conclusion that there is a tendency to a more widespread use of the diminutive in modern Russian.

Obviously in a comparatively short work it is impossible to cover all aspects of this complicated and little studied problem. Many questions connected with the diminutive problem still await a researcher, e.g. the syntactic combinations involving the diminutive, the stylistic use of diminutives, the question of diminutive meaning in the verb, and the analytic means by which diminutive meaning can be expressed.

B. V. B.

---

[1] The problem of the diminutive has interested me for some time and I gratefully accepted the suggestion of Professor D. Ward that I should work on this problem while I was in Edinburgh, where I held an exchange appointment in the Russian Department of Edinburgh University during the academic year 1964–65.

I take advantage of this opportunity to express my sincere thanks to Mr Patrick Waddington, of the University of Belfast, who also intended to write a book on Russian diminutives and who generously shared his observations on this subject with me.

NOTE

This contribution to the series was written in Russian, translated by D. Guild and edited by D. Ward. The editor is responsible for the remarks on stress in the text, and also for the sections on stress and consonant alternations in Appendix 2. The author, translator and editor wish to thank Miss S. White and Rev. J. Sotnikov for typing the several versions which the work has gone through.

1

INTRODUCTION

A. *General remarks on diminutives*

Diminutives are special forms of words derived with the aid of diminutive suffixes, which give to the words the additional meanings of smallness, tenderness, irony, disparagement, i.e. serve as a means of conveying and reinforcing the expressiveness of speech.

Diminutives are to be found in many languages. Languages rich in diminutives are the Slavonic group (especially East Slavonic—Russian, Ukrainian and White Russian), the Baltic group (Lithuanian and Latvian), and the Romance group (especially Italian). In the Germanic group the diminutive is rarer than in the above mentioned. In German there are only two productive diminutive suffixes for the noun, *-lein* (*Büchlein*) and *-chen* (*Händchen*), and for the adjective one, *-lich* (*rundlich*).

In English, diminutives are even rarer than in German. The number of commonly used diminutive forms derived from common nouns is limited to a few dozen words: booklet, flatlet, leaflet, rivulet, streamlet, townlet, kitchenette, laundrette;[1] duckling, gosling, suckling, weakling; grannie, doggie, and some others. Diminutive adjectives are formed in English with the suffix *-ish*: dwarfish, earlyish, greenish, lateish, oldish, youngish, roundish, etc.[2] In former times English (especially Anglo-Saxon) was much richer in diminutive forms (Rotzoll).

The English dialects are richer in diminutives than standard English; the following diminutives are characteristic, for instance, of Scots: bairnie, billie, hillie, housie, kitling, knifie, laddie, lassie,

---

[1] An amusing use of the suffix -ETTE was observed in Edinburgh in the word '*Superette*' over a shop-window—a word consisting only of a prefix and a suffix and apparently meaning 'small super-market'.

[2] As Mr Patrick Waddington (University of Belfast) remarks in a letter to me, ways of expressing diminutive meaning in English 'are not exhausted by the diminutive suffix forms. Perhaps more often used in English are such collocations as *good old, little old* (without the idea of age), or such colloquial expressions in Scotland as "the wee small hours", "she is a sweet wee girl", "that is a brave wee distance", etc.'

lambie, ninnie, pucklie; and there are also some words with a double diminutive suffix: mitherikie, bittikey, housikie, lasseckie, loonikie, pussikie, wifiekie.

The colloquial speech of the area around Aberdeen is notable in this respect. It has even been suggested that the custom of using diminutives may have been brought to this region by one of the Slavonic tribes, the Wends, who could have reached the shores of Scotland and landed around Aberdeen (Bulloch).

We will leave this hypothesis to the conscience of its authors, for it undoubtedly requires much better corroboration than the mere use of the diminutive, and go on to consider the question of the diminutive in Russian.

B. *The diminutive as a means of expression in Russian*

Living Russian is rich in various expressive resources: lexical, grammatical and phonetic. In lexis, it is primarily the very rich word stock and the wide choice of synonyms which constitute the expressive resources; in morphology—the variety of derivatives, including diminutives; in the sphere of syntax—the optimal collocability[1] and relatively free word order; in phonetics—the absence of a limit to the length of stressed vowels and the richness of the intonational resources in conveying the most delicate of emotive and expressive nuances.

Among the most important expressive resources in Russian are *diminutive forms* or simply *diminutives*. In this respect Russian differs essentially from many other languages, including English.

If in English the number of commonly used diminutives (excluding proper names) hardly exceeds a dozen or so, in Russian on the other hand, as preliminary calculations have shown, out of 25,000 of the most commonly used Russian words, more than a thousand nouns and adjectives have or can have diminutive forms. The majority of these are given as examples in this book.

By means of diminutives Russian conveys, among other emotional-expressive nuances, e.g.: the idea of *diminutiveness* (smallness of quantity or size, etc.):

го́род	городо́к	small town
дом	до́мик	small house

[1] 'Collocability' is the range of combinations of a given word with other words (its 'collocations').

ко́мната	ко́мнатка	little room
рука́	ру́чка	small hand
нога́	но́жка	small foot
ка́пля	ка́пелька	small drop, droplet

tenderness:

ми́лый	ми́ленький	nice
сын	сыно́чек	son, small son[1]
дочь	до́чка	daughter, little daughter
дя́дя	дя́денька	uncle, nice uncle
берёза	берёзонька	birch tree, a dear little birch tree
хлеб	хле́бушко	a loaf, a nice little loaf

disparagement:

го́род	городи́шка	a miserable little town
пла́тье	пла́тьишко	a poor sort of dress
жени́х	женишо́к	a sorry-looking bridegroom
актёр	актёришка	a poor sort of actor
поэ́т	поэ́тишка	a poet of sorts

irony:

иде́я	иде́йка	a sort of idea
тео́рия	тео́рийка	a theory
мировоззре́ние	мировоззре́ньице	a way of looking at the world
рабо́тник	рабо́тничек	some worker

condescension and familiarity:

брат	брато́к	some brother
рабо́та	работёночка	work of a sort
племя́нник	племя́нничек	sort of cousin
ко́мната	комнату́шечка	an insignificant little room
ве́щи	вещи́чки	bits and pieces

c. *The range of use of diminutives*

The diminutive is used primarily in the everyday spoken language, in folk poetry and also in some literary styles.

Diminutives are formed in Russian from nouns, adjectives and adverbs. As far as verbs are concerned, diminutives are not typical of this part of speech, though the possibility of expressing diminutiveness is not excluded from some verbal forms (see below). The majority of emotive-expressive forms are to be found in nouns.

Both Russian and English are rich in diminutive forms for

---

[1] Out of a suitable context, and often enough within a context, it is not always possible to convey in English the full flavour of Russian diminutive forms. (Translator.)

proper names. Compare the diminutives of the English name Elizabeth (Eliza, Lizzie, Liz, Betsy, Bessy, Bess, etc.) and the diminutives of the Russian name Мария: Маруся, Марусенька, Марусечка, Маруська, Марийка, Маша, Машенька, Машечка, Машка, Маня, Манечка, Манька, Муся, Мусенька, Мусечка, Муська, Мара, Мура, Мурочка.

Of these, Муська has a suggestion of 'familiarity', while Маруська, Машка, Манька may convey a certain degree of disparagement.

However, the use of diminutives in Russian is far from being restricted to proper nouns; the sphere of diminutive usage covers the following groups of nouns with concrete meaning:

(a) *kinship terms:*

папочка	daddy
мамуся	mummy
дяденька	uncle
сыночек	son

(b) *parts of the body:*

ножка	foot
ручка	hand
головонька	head
глазёнки	eyes

(c) *clothes:*

костюмчик	suit
пальтишко	coat
пиджачок	jacket

(d) *food stuffs:*

хлебушко	a small loaf
мясцо	a small piece of meat
молочко	a little milk
борщец	some borsch

(e) *animals:*

кошечка	a wee cat
собачка	doggie
коровёнка	a small cow
лисонька	a small fox

(f) *trees and plants:*

ёлочка	a small fir
берёзонька	a small birch
травушка	grass

(g) *natural phenomena:*

до́ждичек	a little bit of rain
сне́жо́к	a little bit of snow
ветеро́чек	a slight breeze

(h) *various:*

мину́тка	minute
часо́к	hour
фу́нтик	pound
доми́шко	house
око́нце	window

The use of this or that diminutive in conversation depends on the style and situation (conversation in the family, with children, friends, lovers' talk, etc.), and also on the mood of the speaker, his attitude to the subject of the conversation and on his ability to express his emotion in words. The apposite use of the diminutive requires a certain linguistic training and, in its turn, testifies to a good command of the language.

D. *The meaning of Russian diminutives and their translation into other languages*

If we compare a series of synonyms for 'beautiful' in Russian and English (i.e. in phrases like 'a beautiful child' or 'a beautiful girl') we will probably find that the number of lexical synonyms in both languages is about the same.

However, the Russian adjectives:

краси́вый	beautiful
ми́лый	dear
хоро́ший	fine
сла́вный	grand
чу́дный	splendid

apart from their basic lexical value, inherent also in the corresponding English adjectives, can also convey supplementary emotive-expressive meanings or nuances by forming parallel diminutive forms with the suffix -еньк-: краси́венький, ми́ленький, хоро́шенький, сла́венький, чу́денький. The rendering of similar nuances in English is difficult because of the absence in the latter language of adequate equivalents.

It is, for instance, difficult to decide how best to render into English, keeping as close to the original as possible, the title of

Book I, История одной семейки ('The History of a Family'), of Dostoyevsky's novel Братья Карамазовы (*The Brothers Karamazov*), where the Russian is not simply семьи but семейки—with an ironic, condescending undertone. And yet Russian allows more than one diminutive form for this word, e.g. семеечка or семеюшка, as in Nekrasov's Проснулась вся семеюшка ('The whole family woke up'). How is one to convey all this in English?

The difficulty of explaining and rendering diminutives crops up constantly in modern Soviet literature. Here, for instance, are a few diminutives, with suggested translations, from Shokhov's *Поднятая целина* (*Virgin Soil Upturned*):

милая девчонушка	a nice little girl
начал я копить деньжонок	I began to amass some money
скуповатенькие	on the mean side
улыбался с задумчивой грустинкой	he smiled with a pensive sort of sadness
кто как себя ведёт в этой жизненьке	people behave in different ways in this life

The translation of Russian diminutives is made still more complicated by the fact that Russian nouns and adjectives may have more than one diminutive form. Cf. книга (book), книжка, книжечка, книжоночка, книжонка, книжица—with different emotive-expressive undercurrents:

книжка	(with a nuance of scorn)
книжечка	(diminutive expressing smallness and tenderness)
книжонка	(disparaging diminutive)
книжоночка	(with condescension)
книжица	(with a nuance of irony and condescension)

Russian adjectives may also have two or three diminutive forms with varying degrees of reinforcement of the quality and the nuance of tenderness:

светлый	(light)	светленький; светловатый; светлёхонький;
белый	(white)	беленький; беловатый; белым-белёшенький;
красный	(red)	красненький; красноватый; краснёхонький;

etc.

This diversity of diminutive suffixes is characteristic of Russian. Thus, to form diminutives from nouns more than thirty suffixes are to be found, and from adjectives about ten suffixes. Yet the difficulty of analysing the meanings of diminutives is not confined merely to the great variety of diminutive suffixes, for the fact is that diminutives with one and the same suffix may very often have various shades of meaning—positive or negative—depending on the lexical meaning of the original word, on the context, situation and intonation. For example, diminutives with the suffix -ка can express endearment:

коро́ва	cow	коро́вка
смета́на	sour cream	смета́нка
сторона́	side	сторо́нка

or irony and scorn:

афи́ша	poster	афи́шка
иде́я	idea	иде́йка
семья́	family	семе́йка

The same feature can be observed with diminutives with the suffixes -ик, -чик:

живо́т	stomach	живо́тик (with nuance of tenderness)
винт	screw	ви́нтик (smallness)
студе́нт	student	студе́нтик (scorn)
тип	type	ти́пчик (with nuance of irony)

It should be mentioned that most diminutive suffixes are associated with the rendering of positive emotive-expressive nuances, and only a few are definitely associated with the expression of negative emotions:

-онка/-ёнка:
| | ба́ба | woman | бабёнка |
| | газе́та | newspaper | газетёнка |

-ишко:
| | дом | house | доми́шко |
| | житьё | life | житьи́шко |

-ашка:
| | стари́к | old man | старика́шка |

-ице:
| | мне́ние | opinion | мне́ньице |

and some others.

A particular difficulty is presented by the question of 'degrees of expressiveness', which will be dealt with in greater detail in the next section.

E. *Degrees of diminutiveness in Russian*

A special characteristic of Russian is the stringing together of diminutive suffixes and the formation of diminutives from diminutives with the aim of reinforcing the emotive-expressive meaning, e.g.:

with usual diminutive suffix		*with double diminutive suffix*
мальчи́шка	small boy	мальчи́шечка
мальчо́нка		мальчо́ночка
сестри́ца	little sister	сестри́чка
сестрёнка		сестрёночка
ребёнок	child	ребёночек
котёнок	kitten	котёночек
козлёнок	kid	козлёночек
книжо́нка	small book	книжо́ночка
денёк	day	денёчек
песчи́нка	grain of sand	песчи́ночка

The doubling of the diminutive suffix expresses a greater degree of tenderness, a kindly, loving attitude as in мальчи́шечка, мальчо́ночка, котёночек, сестри́чка, compared with the ordinary diminutives мальчи́шка, котёнок, сестри́ца, which can be emotively neutral or express negative emotions.

The meanings of the remaining diminutive pairs are similarly differentiated, thus:

книжо́нка	has a nuance of scorn while
книжо́ночка	also has this nuance but shows a personal interest in the subject;
денёк	is a stylistic diminutive with a neutral meaning, but sometimes expresses indefiniteness, as in the expression деньќа два 'two days or so' while
денёчек	is an emotively coloured diminutive, as in the expression: Сла́вный был денёчек! ('It was a marvellous day!')

The word песчи́ночка expresses the extreme degree of diminutiveness as well as the concept of 'a single grain'.

Three degrees of expressiveness are distinguished in Russian diminutives: first or minimal, second or intermediate, and third or highest (Vinogradov; Unbegaun).

The first stage of diminutiveness is found in forms containing only one diminutive component:

-ка:	ры́бка	fish
-ик:	до́мик	house
-чик:	журна́льчик	magazine

-ок, -ёк:	дружо́к	friend
	огонёк	light
-це:	зе́ркальце	mirror
-цо:	винцо́	wine
-ице:	ма́слице	butter
-ецо:	письмецо́	letter
-ец:	бра́тец	brother
-ёнок:	тигрёнок	tiger cub
-ёныш:	несмышлёныш	a silly little chap
-ица:	вещи́ца	a small thing
-ыш:	глупы́ш	a silly fellow

Depending on situation and context, different shades of meaning may predominate in diminutives with the minimal degree of expressiveness: mere smallness, tenderness, scorn, irony, familiarity and so on. These nuances can be strengthened by means of the emphatic intonation.

The second degree of expressiveness is associated with diminutives formed with suffixes of heightened expression:

-онька, -енька:	берёзонька	birch-tree
	ре́ченька	stream
-уша, -юша:	дорогу́ша	darling
	Катю́ша	Katie
-ушка:	сосе́душка	neighbour
-онка, -ёнка:	книжо́нка	book
	глазёнки	eyes
-ишка:	вори́шка	thief
-ишко, -ышко:	городи́шко	township
	зёрнышко	grain
-ашка:	старика́шка	little old man

With diminutives of the second degree of expressiveness the hypocoristic[1] nuance predominates and they are rarely used with the meaning of slight scorn or familiarity.

Diminutives of diminutives, formed with the aid of double and sometimes even treble diminutive suffixes, have the third (highest) degree of expressiveness:

-очка:	фигу́рка — фигу́рочка	figure
-очек:	голосо́к — голосо́чек	voice, small voice
-ечка:	ру́чка — ру́чечка	small hand

[1] Henceforth we shall frequently use the technical term 'hypocoristic', meaning by this that the word is diminutive in form (i.e. is formed by means of a diminutive suffix) and expresses an attitude of tenderness or affection without necessarily implying that the object is small in size. Where small size is also clearly implied we shall use the term 'diminutive-hypocoristic'.

-ечко:	словцó — словéчко	word
-оночка:	девчóнка — девчóночка	small girl
-очко:	ведёрко — ведёрочко	small bucket
-урочка:	дóчка — дочýрочка	daughter
-ишечка:	брáтишка — брáтишечка	small brother
-ашечка:	старикáшка — старикáшечка	little old man
-ушечка:	комнатýшка — комнатýшечка	small room
-уленька:	бабýля — бабýленька	a little old woman

Diminutives of the highest degree of expressiveness lose their connection with the meaning of simple diminutiveness and serve as means for expressing positive emotions (love, delight, tender attitudes, etc.). These diminutives are inseparably bound up with the corresponding emphatic intonation.

F. *Tendency for the diminutive to become more widespread in modern Russian literature*

The diminutive has its roots in the colloquial language—especially the folk idiom—from which it spreads into the literary language.

In many literary works diminutives serve as a means of stylization or characterization. The speech of Porfiry Petrovich in Dostoyevsky's *Преступлéние и наказáние*, for example, abounds in ironic diminutives (Mandel'shtam). Many diminutives are to be found in the works of M. E. Saltykov-Shchedrin, in the tales of Chekhov, in the satirical poetry of V. Mayakovsky, in the speech of the characters in Sholokhov's *Пóднятая целинá* and in the works of other writers.

Examination of the works of Russian writers suggests that in modern literature there is a tendency for diminutives to spread and for them to be more frequently used as a means of increased expressiveness.

The Ural tales of P. Bazhov, for instance (*Малахúтовая шкатýлка, Хозя́йка мéдной гáри*, etc.), are especially rich in diminutives. Written in the style of folk speech, these stories contain very rich material for the study of diminutives.

Here are a few examples of the use of diminutives in one of Bazhov's stories:

Вот и рослá та *девчóночка* на примéте у людéй. Самá *чёрненька*, а *глáзки зелёненьки*...
А Танюша стоит *спокойнёшенько*.

And so that little girl grew up, watched over by people. She was dark and green-eyed...
And Tanyusha is standing there so quietly.

Получи́ла *писёмышко.*	She received a letter.
Скорёнько *Таню́шка* всё переняла́.	Tanyusha quickly imitated everything.
Он, знай, *похоха́тывает.*[1]	He just goes on laughing.

Despite the fact that many of these diminutives are not to be found in any dictionary, only the non-Russian reader will have any difficulties in understanding them. The Russian, on the basis of his linguistic experience, interprets these diminutives in their full expressive meaning without any particular difficulty, even when he meets them for the first time.

That the diminutive forms are being further developed and widely used in literature is confirmed too by the numerous examples of their use in Yevgeny Yevtushenko's poem *Бра́тская ГЭС* (1965).

Here is a quatrain from this poem consisting almost entirely of diminutives with ironic undercurrents:

И подбра́сывали *цита́ток*	And they slipped in some quotations
И наро́дного *юморка́*	And some popular humour,
И *бара́нинки* и *цыпля́ток*	Pieces of mutton and chicken
И *огу́рчиков* и *омулька́*	And pieces of cucumber and *omul'*

цита́ток	gen. pl. of	цита́тка	(< цита́та quotation)
юморка́	gen. sg. of	юморо́к	(< ю́мор humour)
бара́нинки	gen. sg. of	бара́нинка	(< бара́нина mutton)
цыпля́ток	gen. pl. of	цыпля́тки	(< цыпля́та chickens)
огу́рчиков	gen. pl. of	огу́рчики	(< огуре́ц cucumber)
омулька́	gen. sg. of	омулёк	(< о́муль fish found only in Lake Baikal)

Among the two hundred diminutives used in the text of this poem, we also come across such rare diminutives as транссиби́рочка, магистра́люшка (транссиби́рская магистра́ль 'Transiberian highway'), etc.[2] The author of the poem makes extensive use of popular speech, and also conversational turns of phrase, where the use of the diminutive is so characteristic.

However, the range of use of diminutives is not confined to the stylization of popular speech or to characterization through dialogue; one can find diminutives throughout a text, even in the author's narrative. Here are a few examples from the story of

---

[1] The general style of the narrative suggests that this is an instance of a verbal diminutive (хохо́чет понемно́жку 'laughs a bit'). See below on verbal diminutives.

[2] Some of these are probably the author's own creations.

M. Alekseyev, *Ýгол óтчий* (*Father's Retreat*), published in *Литературная газета* in the summer of 1965. In the story we have a description of a *tiny little stream* (ма́лая *ре́чушка* [< ре́чка]) which rose *in a bottomless spring* (в бездо́нном *родничке́* [< родни́к]) *and rushed between steep banks* (и кати́лась меж круты́х *бережко́в* [< берега́]), *babbling over stony shallows* (ворча́ на камени́стых *поро́жках* [< поро́ги]). *And its waters were still turbid* (и *води́ца* [< вода́] в ней была́ ещё *мутнёхонька* [< му́тный]). And it was *this tiny, little thing* [э́та са́мая *крохоту́ля* [< кро́хотный]) which flooded the meadows.

Other examples from the same story are: *there flashed now and again rather sly, cunning sparks* (времена́ми вспы́хивали *хитрова́тые* [< хи́трый], лука́вые *огоньки́* [< ого́нь]); *growled at him for some little slip or other* (поворча́л на него́ за каку́ю-то *прома́шку* [< про́мах]); *some will spend all their lives in some little, unknown hamlet* (Ино́й всю жизнь прожива́ет в безве́стном *селе́ньице* [< селе́нье]).

As can be seen from the above examples, modern Russian uses diminutives widely as one of its most important expressive and stylistic resources.

To be able to appreciate properly the beauty and expressiveness of living Russian speech, to have a deep understanding of and to read and translate the works of contemporary Russian literature, with an appreciation of the 'undercurrents', the student of Russian must acquire sufficient knowledge of this important linguistic device—the diminutive. A knowledge of diminutives will, undoubtedly, also help him to develop an intuitive mastery of the spoken language.

G. *The formation of diminutives*

We have already noted that diminutives are formed with the aid of special diminutive suffixes; attached to the basic word these alter its meaning in the direction of greater expressiveness.

In some cases the attaching of diminutive suffixes leads to the formation of new words (new lexemes or lexical units) which detach themselves from the original word and become independent, e.g.:

ру́чка две́ри   door-handle
но́жка стола́   table-leg

нóсик чáйника	teapot spout
кóсточка слúвы	plum-stone
хрустáлик глáза	the lens of the eye

and so on; this is the *word-building* function of diminutive suffixes. In other cases, and this occurs much more frequently in Russian, the diminutive suffixes have the function of form-derivation, i.e. words with the diminutive suffix are derived forms of the basic word, to the meaning of which word they add supplementary expressive nuances: diminutiveness, tenderness, irony and so on.

The meaning of the diminutive word depends in the last count on the interaction of the meaning of the root and the expressive-stylistic meaning of the diminutive suffix (Plyamovataya). Russian has at its disposal a large number of diminutive suffixes with very different shades of meaning. We shall examine in turn the diminutive suffixes of nouns, adjectives and adverbs, primarily from the point of view of the emotive-expressive nuances which these diminutive suffixes give to the diminutive forms, and then we shall dwell briefly on verbal diminutives. Stress and consonant alternations are treated systematically in Appendix 2.

2

DIMINUTIVE SUFFIXES OF NOUNS

Nouns with a concrete meaning have the largest number of diminutive suffixes. Attached to the nominal root, the diminutive suffixes add to the basic meaning of the noun various expressive nuances. Diminutiveness is associated with the feelings of tenderness, kindness, attentiveness and tender emotions in general. This is clearly the reason why the suffixes of purely objective diminutiveness, or those conveying only tenderness, appear comparatively rarely. More frequent are suffixes of a mixed type, combining both diminutive and hypocoristic meanings.

A. *Diminutive suffixes of the first degree of expressiveness*

(i) *The suffix* -ка

This is the most widespread diminutive suffix in Russian. It forms diminutives from feminine nouns. It is interesting to note that nouns with 'subjective evaluation' are more frequently formed from nouns of the feminine gender (Vinogradov, 1947: 146).

The suffix -ка is never stressed. If the original word is itself a derived word, the stress is as in the original word (равни́на — равни́нка). Otherwise the stress falls on the root-syllable (дочь — до́чка, жена́ — жёнка). Note that

(a) when the original word has in the gen. pl. a mobile vowel which occurs in the diminutive, the stress follows that of the gen. pl. (ви́шня — ви́шен — ви́шенка, земля́ — земе́ль — земе́лька, семья́ — семе́й — семе́йка)

and

(b) when the original word has a structure exemplified by such words as голова́, борода́, пелена́, берёза the diminutive has the stress on the syllable before -ка (голо́вка, боро́дка, пелёнка, берёзка).

Usually -ка gives to the word a hypocoristic or diminutive-hypocoristic value, e.g.

вку́сненькая *ка́шка*	tasty porridge (in talking to children)
Хороша́ *земе́лька*	the land is good (with a nuance of enthusiasm)
Ска́зка о рыбаке́ и *ры́бке*	'The Tale of the Fisherman and the Little Fish' (with a definite implication: the story is not going to be about an ordinary fish, but a golden fish)
Кали́нка, кали́нка моя́, в саду́ я́года-*мали́нка* моя́	'My guelder-rose, my guelder-rose and my raspberries in the garden' (hypocoristic terms for bushes, in a popular song)
голо́вка, но́жка, ру́чка	head, foot, hand (diminutive-hypocoristic, referring to a child's head, etc.)

Depending on the situation and the context the hypocoristic nuance may predominate in some cases and that of diminutiveness in others. The following diminutives in -ка are used with hypocoristic meaning:

бара́нина	mutton	бара́нинка
ба́сня	fable	ба́сенка
ви́шня	cherry	ви́шенка
дочь	daughter	до́чка

жена́	wife	жёнка
змея́	snake	зме́йка
коро́ва	cow	коро́вка
котле́та	cutlet	котле́тка
льди́на	ice-floe	льди́нка
мину́та	minute	мину́тка
мышь	mouse	мы́шка
неде́ля	week	неде́лька
ночь	night	но́чка
пе́сня	song	пе́сенка
пчела́	bee	пчёлка
пшени́ца	wheat	пшени́чка[1]
ряби́на	rowan-tree	ряби́нка
свини́на	pork	свини́нка
сигаре́та	cigarette	сигаре́тка
смета́на	sour cream	смета́нка
сморо́дина	currants	сморо́динка
спа́льня	bedroom	спа́ленка
стару́ха	old woman	стару́шка
сторона́	side	сторо́нка
страни́ца	page	страни́чка
теля́тина	veal	теля́тинка
трава́	grass	тра́вка
фигу́ра	figure	фигу́рка
ха́та	hut	ха́тка
чере́шня	cherry	чере́шенка
черни́ка	bilberries	черни́чка
шту́ка	thing	шту́чка
штуко́вина	thing	штуко́винка
шу́ба	fur coat	шу́бка
щети́на	bristle	щети́нка
щу́ка	pike	щу́чка

The following words are most frequently used with the meaning of diminutiveness:

апте́ка	chemist's	апте́чка
библиоте́ка	library	библиоте́чка
брошю́ра	brochure	брошю́рка
высота́	height	высо́тка
гора́	mountain	го́рка
доли́на	valley	доли́нка
доро́га	way	доро́жка
ель	fir	ёлка
жи́ла	vein	жи́лка
кана́ва	ditch	кана́вка
кастрю́ля	casserole	кастрю́лька
ко́мната	room	ко́мнатка
крова́ть	bed	крова́тка

[1] For consonant changes see Appendix 2.

ку́ча	heap	ку́чка
морщи́на	wrinkle	морщи́нка
нора́	burrow	но́рка
пери́на	eiderdown	пери́нка
поля́на	glade	поля́нка
равни́на	plain	равни́нка
ра́на	wound	ра́нка
река́	river	ре́чка
струя́	jet	стру́йка
сце́на	scene	сце́нка
табли́ца	table	табли́чка
тетра́дь	jotter	тетра́дка
тропа́	path	тро́пка
шку́ра	skin	шку́рка
шля́па	hat	шля́пка
што́ра	blind	што́рка
щепо́ть	pinch	щепо́тка

The following diminutives in -ка are used with the meaning of irony and familiarity:

ава́рия	accident	ава́рийка
актри́са	actress	актри́ска
афи́ша	poster	афи́шка
газе́та	newspaper	газе́тка
дисципли́на	discipline	дисципли́нка
иде́я	idea	иде́йка
кни́га	book	кни́жка
меда́ль	medal	меда́лька
рабо́та	work	рабо́тка
семья́	family	семе́йка

The following forms with the suffix -ка, given here with the original words, have become independent words:

ви́лы	pitchfork	ви́лка	fork
гре́бень	crest	гребёнка (N.B. stress)	comb
голова́	head	голо́вка	head (e.g. of a pin, bulb, onion)[1]
игла́	needle	иго́лка	needle[2]
каби́на	cabin	каби́нка	cabin[3]

[1] Also diminutive of голова́.
[2] Both игла́ and иго́лка (which is not diminutive in meaning) mean a 'needle for sewing', whereas in all other meanings (knitting-needle, gramophone-needle, pine-needle, etc.) only игла́ is used.
[3] Каби́нка may be used as a diminutive to каби́на or may be a simple equivalent, with no diminutive meaning. In some contexts one form is preferred to the other, e.g. каби́нка на пля́же 'beach-hut'.

доро́га	road	доро́жка	strip of carpet
карти́на	picture	карти́нка	illustration
кора́	bark of a tree, crust of the earth	ко́рка	crust of bread
корзи́на	basket	корзи́нка	small basket, punnet
за́навес	curtain (in a theatre)	занаве́ска (N.B. stress)	curtain (in a house)
каре́та	carriage	каре́тка	carriage of a typewriter
коло́нна	column	коло́нка	geyser
коро́на	crown	коро́нка	crown of a tooth
кро́хи	remains, fragments, crumbs[1]	кро́шка	crumb[2]
кры́ша	roof	кры́шка	lid, e.g. of a pan
ку́кла	doll	ку́колка	chrysalis, pupa
маши́на	machine	маши́нка	typewriter
нить	thread	ни́тка	thread[3]
нога́	leg	но́жка	leg, e.g. of a table
печь	stove, furnace	пе́чка	stove[4]
пласти́на	plate	пласти́нка	record
плита́	stove	пли́тка	tile
рука́	hand	ру́чка	handle, e.g. of a door
сеть	net	се́тка	net[5]
скамья́	bench	скаме́йка	bench, seat[6]
стрела́	arrow	стре́лка	hand of a watch
ступе́нь	step, rung	ступе́нька	step, rung[7]
ча́ша	chalice	ча́шка	cup

[1] In figurative sense.
[2] In literal sense, e.g. bread-crumbs.
[3] Ни́тка means a thread of cotton, etc., while нить, though it may sometimes have this sense, is commoner in the sense of 'thread-like object' (не́рвные ни́ти 'nerve-threads') or in a figurative sense (нить разгово́ра 'the thread of a conversation').
[4] Пе́чка signifies only a stove for heating a room, whereas печь is used in this and other senses (e.g. до́менная печь 'blast-furnace', плави́льная печь 'smelting furnace').
[5] Both сеть and се́тка mean a net for catching things, a small net (e.g. a butterfly-net) usually being called се́тка. Otherwise, the words differentiate various kinds of 'nets' (e.g. игра́ у се́тки 'net play', железнодоро́жная сеть 'railway network').
[6] Both скамья́ and скаме́йка mean a bench for sitting on, скаме́йка being commoner in this sense. In figurative usage (e.g. 'the bench' in the sense of a judge or judges) only скамья́ is used.
[7] Ступе́нька may act as a diminutive to ступе́нь or may be simply an equivalent, in the sense of a rung or a step on a stair. In the non-physical sense of 'stage in the development of' ступе́нь is used (вы́сшая ступе́нь капитали́зма 'the highest stage of capitalism'). The use of ступе́нька in a non-physical sense is *figurative* and the word then has diminutive meaning.

(ii) *The suffix* -ик

This is one of the most productive suffixes in modern Russian. It forms diminutives from masculine nouns. Together with the meaning of diminutiveness, forms in -ик (especially when talking to children) evoke the emotive colourings of tenderness, kindness or endearment. Thus, the forms бра́тик (< брат), го́дик (< год) and зу́бик (< зуб) convey the ideas of smallness and tenderness in the speech of children or when talking to children, as in

Моему́ *бра́тику* уже́ *го́дик*, у него́ проре́зался *зу́бик*	My brother is already a year old, and he's cut a tooth

The form биле́тик (< биле́т) in

Купи́те *биле́тик*!	Do buy a ticket

does not mean a small ticket (the ticket may be of the usual dimensions) but adds an emotional nuance, suggesting: 'Be so kind as to buy...' The forms све́тик (< свет 'light') and соко́лик (< соко́л[1] 'falcon') are used as terms of endearment by a mother to a son, for example, or a woman to the man she loves, as in све́тик мой, соко́лик.

This suffix is not stressed. In nearly all instances, the stress in the diminutive falls on the same syllable as in the nom. sing. of the original noun. Exceptions are noted below.

The following diminutives with the suffix -ик are used predominantly with hypocoristic meaning:

анана́с	pineapple	анана́сик
буфе́т	sideboard	буфе́тик
велосипе́д	bicycle	велосипе́дик
живо́т	belly	живо́тик
каранда́ш	pencil	каранда́шик
кот	cat	ко́тик
лоб	forehead	ло́бик
матро́с	sailor	матро́сик
мяч	ball	мя́чик
парово́з	steam locomotive	парово́зик
парохо́д	steamboat	парохо́дик
огуре́ц	cucumber	огу́рчик[2]
сад	garden	са́дик
суп	soup	су́пик
хвост	tail	хво́стик
чиж	siskin	чи́жик

[1] The literary form is now со́кол.

[2] For consonant changes see Appendix 2. Note that the stress is on у, since the е of the original word is not in the diminutive.

However, the chief meaning of the majority of diminutives in -ик is smallness, e.g.:

аппара́т	apparatus	аппара́тик
винт	screw	ви́нтик
гара́ж	garage	гара́жик
гвоздь	nail	гво́здик
двор	courtyard	дво́рик
дом	house	до́мик
заво́д	factory	заво́дик
кана́т	rope	кана́тик
ключ	key	клю́чик
ковёр	carpet	ко́врик[1]
кран	tap	кра́ник
куст	bush	ку́стик
мост	bridge	мо́стик
нож	knife	но́жик
паке́т	packet	паке́тик
стол	table	сто́лик
сугро́б	snow-drift	сугро́бик
таз	basin	та́зик
том	volume	то́мик
торт	cake	то́ртик
хала́т	dressing-gown	хала́тик
холм	hill	хо́лмик
хрящ	gristle	хря́щик
шарф	scarf	ша́рфик
шрам	scar	шра́мик
штамп	punch/die	шта́мпик

A whole series of words with the diminutive suffix -ик may take on the meaning of ironic familiarity, slight scorn or disparagement, insignificance, or may be used in an ingratiating manner, e.g.:

Получи́л *ава́нсик* [< ава́нс]	I received a small [insignificant] advance of money
На́добно соста́вить *а́ктик* [< акт]	A statement will have to be drawn up [may be ironical or ingratiating]
Э́тот *пу́нктик* [< пункт] на́до бы включи́ть	This small point should be mentioned [ironic disparagement]

Diminutives used with the aforementioned nuances are in the main formed from words of foreign origin, which predominate in the following list:

агрега́т	aggregate	агрега́тик
акце́нт	accent	акце́нтик
анекдо́т	anecdote	анекдо́тик
аргуме́нт	argument	аргуме́нтик
аттеста́т	certificate	аттеста́тик

[1] N.B. stress on o, since the e of the original word is not in the suffix.

афори́зм	aphorism	афори́змик
бага́ж	luggage	бага́жик
бюдже́т	budget	бюдже́тик
деса́нт	landing	деса́нтик
докуме́нт	document	докуме́нтик
жест	gesture	же́стик
инциде́нт	incident	инциде́нтик
отчёт	account	отчётик
отка́з	refusal	отка́зик
пакт	pact	па́ктик
пате́нт	patent	пате́нтик
пейза́ж	landscape	пейза́жик
приве́т	greetings	приве́тик
прика́з	order	прика́зик
проце́нт	percentage	проце́нтик
рубль	rouble	ру́блик
тип	type	ти́пик
стаж	length of service	ста́жик
студе́нт	student	студе́нтик
тост	toast	то́стик
фабрика́нт	manufacturer	фабрика́нтик
фильм	film	фи́льмик
фунт	pound	фу́нтик
шанс	chance	ша́нсик
эпизо́д	episode	эпизо́дик
эта́п	stage	эта́пик

In the following phrases words with the diminutive suffix -ик have lost their diminutive significance:

ва́лик пи́шущей маши́ны	the platen of the typewriter (cf. вал 'shaft')
ко́вшик для воды́	a water scoop (cf. ковш 'ladle')
капита́нский *мо́стик*	the captain's bridge (cf. мост 'bridge')
карма́нный *но́жик*	a pocket knife (cf. нож 'knife')
но́сик ча́йника	the spout of a teapot (cf. нос 'nose')
туале́тный *сто́лик*	a dressing-table (cf. стол 'table')
хому́тик винто́вки	backsight/slide of a rifle (cf. хому́т 'collar')
хруста́лик гла́за	lens of eye (cf. хруста́ль 'crystal')
кровяны́е *ша́рики*	blood corpuscles (cf. шар 'sphere')

The change of ц to ч (огуре́ц — огу́рчик, p. 18) is also exemplified by счастли́вец ('lucky man') — счастли́вчик, краса́вец ('handsome man') — краса́вчик, люби́мец ('favourite') — люби́мчик ('favourite', i.e. one favoured to the disadvantage of others). In such words the suffix is -ик, not -чик, which now follows.

(iii) *The suffix* -чик

This productive suffix is added to masculine nouns ending in в, л, м, н, р, й, and is an offshoot of the suffix -ик. The range of meaning which is found with the suffix -ик is also characteristic of the suffix -чик. The stress is as in the original word.

The following are used with a predominantly hypocoristic or diminutive-hypocoristic meaning:

апельси́н	orange	апельси́нчик
бара́н	ram	бара́нчик
бензи́н	petrol	бензи́нчик
дива́н	divan	дива́нчик
журна́л	magazine	журна́льчик
килогра́мм	kilogramme	килогра́мчик
костю́м	suit	костю́мчик
лимо́н	lemon	лимо́нчик
магази́н	shop	магази́нчик
нейло́н	nylon	нейло́нчик
патефо́н	gramophone	патефо́нчик
прибо́р	instrument	прибо́рчик
трамва́й	tram	трамва́йчик

In the following the meaning of smallness is predominant:

автомоби́ль	car	автомоби́льчик
аэродро́м	aerodrome	аэродро́мчик
балко́н	balcony	балко́нчик
бока́л	goblet	бока́льчик
ваго́н	carriage	ваго́нчик
газо́н	lawn	газо́нчик
жето́н	counter	жето́нчик
забо́р	fence	забо́рчик
капюшо́н	hood	капюшо́нчик
карма́н	pocket	карма́нчик
кинжа́л	dagger	кинжа́льчик
коридо́р	corridor	коридо́рчик
мото́р	motor	мото́рчик
павильо́н	pavilion	павильо́нчик
резервуа́р	reservoir	резервуа́рчик
сара́й	shed	сара́йчик
тало́н	coupon	тало́нчик
фонта́н	fountain	фонта́нчик
фурго́н	van	фурго́нчик
чемода́н	trunk	чемода́нчик

The following have a nuance of irony and familiarity:

бюллете́нь	bulletin	бюллете́нчик
гекта́р	hectare	гекта́рчик
гонора́р	fee	гонора́рчик
господи́н	mister	господи́нчик
диапазо́н	range	диапазо́нчик
жарго́н	slang	жарго́нчик
изъя́н	flaw	изъя́нчик
моти́в	motive	моти́вчик
приём	method	приёмчик
прогу́л	shirking	прогу́льчик
рома́н	novel	рома́нчик
семина́р	seminar	семина́рчик
тип	type	ти́пчик
филиа́л	branch	филиа́льчик
экземпля́р	copy	экземпля́рчик

The following have lost their diminutive meaning:

балло́н	gas-container	балло́нчик	gas-cartridge, pellet for soda-water bottle
бараба́н	drum	бараба́нчик	(small) drum[1]
блин	pancake	бли́нчик	pancake as a *sweet* dish
ко́локол	bell	колоко́льчик (N.B. stress)	door-bell, harness-bell, etc.
ларь	bin, chest, booth	ла́рчик	box
ма́лый	lad, youth	ма́льчик	boy

(iv) *The suffix* -ок/-ёк

This suffix is used with nouns of the masculine gender, giving them a diminutive-hypocoristic meaning or one of irony or disparagement. It is one of the oldest Russian diminutive suffixes. At the present time it is of low productivity as it is being supplanted by the suffix -ик. Compare домо́к — до́мик (< дом 'house'), листо́к — ли́стик (< лист 'leaf'), разо́к — ра́зик (< раз 'time'), рото́к — ро́тик (< рот 'mouth'), часо́к — ча́сик (< час 'hour'). In the nom. sing. the stress falls on the mobile vowel о/ё, in all other cases on the ending, thus ветеро́к — ветерка́.

Examples of this suffix are:

(*a*) with hypocoristic meaning or, in some instances, diminutive-hypocoristic meaning:

ве́тер	breeze	ветеро́к
го́вор	dialect	говоро́к

[1] As part of a machine.

го́лос	voice	голосо́к
го́род	town	городо́к
день	day	денёк
друг	friend	дружо́к[1]
дуб	oak	дубо́к
земля́к	fellow countryman	землячо́к
каблу́к	heel	каблучо́к
коньа́к	cognac	коньячо́к
лес	wood	лесо́к
луг	meadow	лужо́к
мёд	honey	медо́к
но́готь	nail	ногото́к[2]
ого́нь	fire	огонёк
о́стров	island	острово́к
па́рень	boy	паренёк
пасту́х	shepherd	пастушо́к
пень	stump	пенёк
пету́х	cock	петушо́к
по́яс	belt	поясо́к
пух	down	пушо́к
пята́к	five copeck piece	пятачо́к
рог	horn	рожо́к
ручѐй	brook	ручеёк (gen. ручейка́)
ряд	row	рядо́к
стари́к	old man	старичо́к
таба́к	tobacco	табачо́к
творо́г	curds	творожо́к
у́голь	coal	уголёк
флаг	flag	флажо́к
чай	tea	чаёк (gen. чайка́)
шёпот	whisper	шепото́к
шум	noise	шумо́к
ячме́нь	barley	ячменёк

(b) with the meaning of irony or disparagement:

брак	marriage	брачо́к
дура́к	fool	дурачо́к
жени́х	fiancé	женишо́к
жир	fat	жиро́к
зять	son-in-law	зятёк
князь	prince	князёк
коро́ль	king	королёк
о́рден	order	орденёк
о́рдер	warrant	ордеро́к
особня́к	private house	особнячо́к

[1] Velar consonants (к, г, х) undergo mutation before this suffix (see Appendix 2).
[2] N.B. hard т.

простак	simpleton		простачок	
пустяк	nonsense		пустячок	
смех	laughter		смешок	
царь	tsar		царёк	

The following have acquired independent meanings, though some of them (marked with an asterisk in the following list) may still occur with diminutive function:

бачок	bin for rubbish	(cf.	бак	tank)
волосок*	hair-spring	(cf.	волос	hair)
глазок*[1]	peep-hole; eye in potato	(cf.	глаз	eye)
грибок*	fungus; mushroom for darning	(cf.	гриб	mushroom)
жучок*	wood engraver[2] (kind of beetle)	(cf.	жук	beetle)
значок	badge	(cf.	знак	sign)
зрачок	pupil (of eye)	(cf.	зрак	gaze)
конёк*	hobby-horse	(cf.	конь	horse)
котелок	bowler-hat	(cf.	котёл	boiler)
кусок	piece	(cf.	кус	bite)
мешок	bag	(cf.	мех	fur)
молоток	hammer, mallet	(cf.	молот	hammer)
носок	sock	(cf.	нос	nose)
пузырёк	phial	(cf.	пузырь	bubble)
садок	fish-tank	(cf.	сад	garden)
уголок*	corner[3]	(cf.	угол	corner)
узелок	bundle	(cf.	узел	knot)
язычок	uvula	(cf.	язык	tongue)

(v) *The suffix* -(e)цо/-(и)це

This suffix forms diminutives from neuter nouns. These diminutives either have simple diminutive meaning or, more often, hypocoristic meaning.

If the stem of the original noun is stressed, then the diminutive has the same stress and the ending -e, otherwise this suffix is stressed -(e)цо́. There are some exceptions. After a single consonant in the stem the form of the suffix is -цо or -це, otherwise it is -ецо or -ице. Note that the soft sign before a vowel letter indicates the occurrence of the consonant j before the vowel. Hence in, e.g. бельецо́, there are two consonants at the end of the stem and therefore the suffix takes the form -ецо, the stress being on the ending—[bilji'tso]. Examples are:

---

[1] As a *diminutive*, has plural глазки, gen. глазок.
[2] Also, colloquially, a home-made electric fuse.
[3] As in Красный уголок 'Red Corner'—a club-room for political, recreational or educational purposes.

бельё	linen; underclothes	бельецо́
боло́то	marsh	боло́тце
вино́	wine	винцо́
де́рево	tree	деревцо́
зе́ркало	mirror	зе́ркальце
зо́лото	gold	зо́лотце
ма́сло	butter	ма́слице
одея́ло	blanket	одея́льце
ожере́лье	necklace	ожере́льице
окно́	window	око́нце
пальто́	coat	пальтецо́
пи́во	beer	пивцо́
пече́нье	biscuit	пече́ньице
письмо́	letter	письмецо́
ружьё	rifle	ружьецо́
са́ло	suet	са́льце
селе́нье	village	селе́ньице
сло́во	word	словцо́

The form -ице is also often used to form diminutives with an ingratiating or 'obliging' purpose. This ingratiating style was widespread in the pre-revolutionary official milieu and was reflected in the literature of the nineteenth century. Examples are:

Обрати́те *внима́ньице*   Please pay attention
На́до пода́ть *заявле́ньице*   You must submit an application

Further examples of such diminutives, with the form -ице of the suffix, are:

жела́ние	desire	жела́ньице
зада́ние	task	зада́ньице
заведе́ние	institution	заведе́ньице
затрудне́ние	difficulty	затрудне́ньице
изде́лие	product	изде́льице
изрече́ние	saying	изрече́ньице
помеще́ние	lodging	помеще́ньице
состоя́ние	state	состоя́ньице
сча́стье	happiness	сча́стьице
телосложе́ние	figure	телосложе́ньице

Diminutives with the suffixal form -ице are rarer in the modern language. They serve as a means of stylization and are used for various expressive purposes, including rather ingratiating politeness:

Как здоро́вьице?   How's your health?
Как настрое́ньице?   What kind of mood are you in?

(vi) *The suffix* -ец

This suffix is most often used to form diminutives with hypocoristic meaning, though it can also form diminutives with the nuance of disparagement.

If the original word has a stress-shift in any of its forms, then the stress falls on the suffix -ец in the nom.-acc. and on the ending in all other cases. If the original word has no stress-shift, then the stress in the diminutive is on the same syllable as in the original word. The e of this suffix is a mobile vowel, hence брáтец—gen. sing. брáтца.

Examples are:

hypocoristic:

алмáз	diamond	алмáзец
брат	brother	брáтец
мáлый	lad	малéц
морóз	frost	морóзец
нарóд	people, nation	нарóдец
хлеб	bread, loaf	хлéбец

Note also щец, a hypocoristic gen. pl. of щи 'cabbage soup'.

disparaging:

анекдóт	anecdote	анекдóтец
закáз	order	закáзец
капитáл	capital	капитáлец

The diminutive suffix -ец is not very productive; forms in -ец are being supplanted by forms in -ик, -чик. Cf.

билéтец	ticket	билéтик
букéтец	bouquet	букéтик
залúвец	bay	залúвик

The low productivity of the diminutive suffix -ец is perhaps to be explained by homonymy (coincidence) of suffixes, since there exists a parallel suffix -ец, which is found in many words and is not a diminutive suffix:

дéло	matter	делéц	smart dealer
молодóй	young	молодéц	fine fellow
нáглый	impudent	наглéц	impudent person
пóдлый	mean, base	подлéц	scoundrel
хрáбрый	brave	храбрéц	brave, courageous man
шельмá	rogue	шельмéц	rogue

(vii) *The suffixes* -ёнок/-онок, *and* -ёныш

These are normally used in words signifying the young of animals; diminutives with these suffixes are always masculine, though they may be derived from feminine or neuter words (e.g. мышь, дитя). The more productive of these two suffixes is -ёнок/-онок (where the second vowel is mobile):

буйвол	buffalo	буйволёнок	buffalo calf
козёл	goat	козлёнок	kid
кот	cat	котёнок	kitten
медведь	bear	медвежонок	bear cub
мышь	mouse	мышонок	mouse
орёл	eagle	орлёнок	eaglet
тигр	tiger	тигрёнок	tiger cub
гад	reptile	гадёнок	reptile
дитя	child	детёныш	young of an animal (N.B. vowel-change)
зверь	wild animal	зверёныш	wild animal
змея	snake	змеёныш	snake
гусь	goose	гусёныш	gosling

Note also:

| несмышлёный | slow-witted | несмышлёныш | a silly little chap |

The suffix -ёнок/-онок and its derivative -чонок are also used to form the nouns denoting children:

внук	grandson	внучонок	grandchild (N.B. consonant change)
повар	cook	поварёнок	cook's child
китаец	Chinese	китайчонок	Chinese child (N.B. consonant change)
татарин	Tartar	татарчонок	Tartar child
цыган	gypsy	цыганёнок	gypsy child

Diminutives with the suffix -ёнок/-онок are used with a purely diminutival meaning; they may be neutral as far as expressiveness is concerned, or they may acquire in the context a hypocoristic nuance. Diminutives with the suffix -ёныш may be neutral or they may express a negative emotion. It is interesting to note that diminutives with a neutral meaning may have derivatives with the hypocoristic nuance:

котёнок	kitten	котёночек
мышонок	mouse	мышоночек
внучонок	grandchild	внучоночек

while diminutives with a negative meaning cannot take supplementary suffixes.

(viii) *The suffix* -ица

This is used in words of feminine gender predominantly with the meaning of diminutiveness. It is non-productive.

In the diminutives formed from nouns ending in stressed -а/-я or in the soft sign the suffix is stressed -и́ца, otherwise the stress falls on the same syllable as in the original word.

Examples are:

вещь	thing	вещи́ца
земля́	land	земли́ца
ка́ша	porridge	ка́шица
ко́жа	skin	ко́жица
крупа́	groats, meal	крупи́ца
лу́жа	puddle	лу́жица
про́сьба	request	про́сьбица
ро́жа	ugly mug	ро́жица
сестра́	sister	сестри́ца

The word части́ца ('particle'), derived from часть ('part') has acquired independent meaning (cf. фи́зика элемента́рных части́ц—'the physics of elementary particles').

(ix) *The suffix* -инка

This suffix produces feminine nouns from original feminines or masculines. It is both singulative (expressing *one* of a mass) and diminutive, and is productive. The stress is usually on the suffix, -и́нка, but there are some exceptions.

изю́м	raisins	изю́минка	a raisin
ко́фе	coffee	кофе́йнка	a coffee-grain
крупа́	groats, meal	крупи́нка	a grain
песо́к	sand	песчи́нка	grit, grain of sand (N.B. consonant change)
пух	down	пуши́нка	a bit of fluff (N.B. consonant change)
пыль	dust	пыли́нка	a grain of dust
снег	snow	снежи́нка	a snow-flake (N.B. consonant change)
соло́ма	straw	соло́минка	a straw
сор	litter	сори́нка	a mote
чай	tea	чаи́нка	a tea-leaf

Note also:

чепуха́	nonsense	чепуши́нка	a piece of nonsense (N.B. consonant change)

An identical suffix -инка produces from adjectives a few nouns with a diminutive nuance and having a limited range of use:

го́рький	bitter	горчи́нка	slightly bitter taste
ки́слый	sour, acid	кисли́нка	
		as in	
		с кисли́нкой	tart, sourish

(x) *The suffix* -ыш

This suffix imparts to masculine diminutives formed from adjectives or participles an expressive colouring of familiarity and tenderness or sympathy, though it may also produce words with a disparaging sense. Many words formed with this suffix denote children. It is non-productive. If the original word has final stress in any of its forms, then the stress usually falls on the suffix -ыш in the nom.-acc. and on the ending in all other cases. Otherwise the stress is as in the original word.

Examples are:

глу́пый	stupid	глупы́ш	a silly little thing
заморённый	emaciated	заморы́ш	puny creature
ма́лый	small	малы́ш	kid
кре́пкий	strong	крепы́ш	a robust fellow, sturdy child
приёмный	foster[1]	приёмыш	adopted child, foster child
подки́нутый	abandoned	подки́дыш[2]	waif

(xi) *The suffixes* -ко *and* -ико

By means of the suffix -ко, which appears to be no longer productive, a dozen or so diminutives have been created from neuter nouns, such as

| ведро́ | bucket | ведёрко |
| о́зеро | lake | озерко́ |

and, with mutation to ч of к in the original word,

о́блако	cloud	о́блачко
я́блоко	apple	я́блочко
яйцо́	egg	яи́чко

The position of the stress appears to be unpredictable.

The mutation of ц to ч, together with the inserted vowel е can give rise to the impression that a word has been formed by means of a double diminutive suffix, as in

| кольцо́ | ring | коле́чко |
| крыльцо́ | porch | крыле́чко |

[1] As in приёмный оте́ц 'foster-father'.
[2] N.B. the д is found in the simple verb кида́ть 'to throw', 'to abandon' and in the impfv. подки́дывать.

In three neuter diminutives the non-productive suffix -ико occurs:

колесо́	wheel	колёсико
лицо́	face	ли́чико
плечо́	shoulder	пле́чико

One should also note the unique form око́шко, a diminutive form from окно́ 'window'.

(xii) *The suffix* -ца

There are a few diminutives with the suffix -ца (always stressed), formed from feminine nouns ending in -ь or -ота. The suffix -ца is either no longer productive or has a very weak potential of productivity. Diminutives of this type, which are found principally in colloquial style, may convey a nuance of disparagement:

грязь	dirt	грязца́
лень	laziness	ленца́
пыль	dust	пыльца́
хрипота́	hoarseness	хрипотца́

B. *Diminutive suffixes of the second degree of expressiveness*

(i) *The suffix* -енька

This productive suffix is used to form diminutives with hypocoristic significance from both masculine and feminine nouns, the stress being on the syllable before the suffix:

ба́тя	dad	ба́тенька
доро́га	road	доро́женька
дочь	daughter	до́ченька
душа́	heart, darling	ду́шенька
дя́дя	uncle	дя́денька
ма́ма	mummy	ма́менька
па́па	papa	па́пенька
тётя	aunt	тётенька
тя́тя	dad	тя́тенька

The suffix -енька is also used to derive terms of endearment from proper names, usually from diminutives of the first degree of expressiveness:

Full name		Diminutive of the first degree of expressiveness	Diminutive of the second degree of expressiveness
Александр	Alexander	Саша	Сашенька
Анатолий	Anatole	Толя	Толенька
Борис	Boris	Боря	Боренька
Виктор	Victor	Витя	Витенька
Владимир	Vladimir	Володя[1]	Володенька
Григорий	Gregory	Гриша	Гришенька
Дмитрий	Dmitry	Митя	Митенька
Екатерина	Katherine	Катя	Катенька
Илья	Elias	Илюша	Илюшенька
Константин	Constantine	Костя	Костенька
Мария	Mary	Маруся	Марусенька
Михаил	Michael	Миша	Мишенька
Надежда	Hope	Надя	Наденька
Николай	Nicholas	Коля	Коленька
Павел	Paul	Павлуша	Павлушенька
Пётр	Peter	Петя	Петенька
Сергей	Serge	Серёжа	Серёженька
Яков	James	Яша	Яшенька

(ii) *The suffix* -онька

This is also used in masculine and feminine diminutives with hypocoristic meaning. The stress falls on the syllable before the suffix:

берёза	birch	берёзонька
дева	girl	девонька
детка	child	детонька
киса	puss	кисонька
лапа	paw	лапонька

In proper names, after soft consonants and ш, ж, the suffix -енька is used (see above), whereas after hard consonants (other than ш and ж) the suffix -онька is used:

Елизавета	Elizabeth	Лиза	Лизонька
Зинаида	Zinaida	Зина	Зинонька
Ирина	Irene	Ира	Иронька
Лидия	Lydia	Лида	Лидонька
София	Sophia	Софа	Софонька
Юрий	Yury	Юра	Юронька

[1] Володя is derived from the native Old Russian form Володимир whereas Владимир is the Old Church Slavonic version of the same name.

(iii) *The suffix* -ушка/-юшка (*and* -ушко/-юшко)

This suffix is used mainly in feminine nouns, less commonly in masculine and neuter nouns (in the last case it takes the form -ушко/-юшко—see below). It conveys endearment, a kindly attitude, sometimes jocularity. The stress usually falls on the syllable before the suffix.[1]

The suffix -ушка/-юшка is fairly productive:

бáба	woman	бáбушка (grandmother)
вдовá	widow	вдóвушка
вóля	will	вóлюшка
головá	head	голóвушка
дед	grandfather	дéдушка
дубúна	cudgel	дубúнушка
дя́дя	uncle	дя́дюшка
женá	wife	жёнушка
зимá	winter	зúмушка
избá	hut	избýшка
кóмната	room	комнатýшка
мать	mother	мáтушка
невéста	bride	невéстушка
рабóта	work	рабóтушка
рекá	river	рéчушка (see below)
смерть	death	смéртушка
соловéй	nightingale	солóвушка
сосéд	neighbour	сосéдушка
тётя	aunt	тётушка

Note the stress in избýшка and комнатýшка and that besides the hypocoristic рéчушка there is a diminutive, usually with a nuance of disparagement, речýшка.

The suffix -ушко is found in a few diminutives characteristic of dialect speech and the style of folklore, with the nuance of increased expressiveness:

гóре	grief	гóрюшко
мóре	sea	мóрюшко
раздóлье	expanse	раздóлюшко
хлеб	bread	хлéбушко

[1] Such diminutives as болтýшка, хохотýшка are derived, by means of the suffix -ка, with change of х to ш, from words ending in -уха (болтýшка < болтýнья, 'chatterbox', хохотýха < хохотýнья, 'merry woman'). Note also that the following forms in -ýшка are not diminutives: волнýшка 'coral milky cap' (kind of mushroom); восьмýшка 'eighth, octavo'; горбýшка 'crust, end of loaf'; полýшка 'a quarter copeck'; телýшка 'heifer'; теплýшка 'heated waggon or hut'; etc.

(iv) *The suffix* -уша/-юша

This suffix is not productive. It is always stressed, forms a few diminutives from proper names:

Илья́	Elias	Илью́ша
Ка́тя	Kate	Катю́ша
Па́вел	Paul	Павлу́ша

and a few diminutives of endearment from nouns and adjectives, which have, however, a dialect flavour, such as:

дорого́й	dear	дорогу́ша	darling
копу́н	'slow-coach'	копу́ша	
ми́лый	dear	милу́ша	darling
родно́й	dear	родну́ша	darling

A few such words in -уша are not diminutives at all.

(v) *The suffix* -ышко (*and* -ышек)

This suffix is used to form diminutives from neuter nouns. Such diminutives are hypocoristic or diminutive-hypocoristic. The stress falls on the syllable before the suffix:

бревно́	log	брёвнышко
ведро́	bucket	вёдрышко
гнездо́	nest	гнёздышко
го́рло	throat	го́рлышко
зерно́	grain	зёрнышко
крыло́	wing	кры́лышко
пятно́	spot	пя́тнышко
со́лнце	sun	со́лнышко

Words with the suffix -ышко are typical of the colloquial language and works of folklore. The suffix is of low productivity.

One or two masculine nouns have diminutives formed with the associated suffix -ышек:

воробе́й	sparrow	воро́бышек
кол	stake	ко́лышек

(vi) *The suffixes* -ишко *and* -ишка

These fairly productive suffixes are used principally to derive diminutives from masculine and neuter nouns. Such diminutives convey disparagement or a condescending irony.

If the stress in the original word is on the endings or passes on to the endings in any of its forms, then the stress in the diminutive falls on the suffix, otherwise it is usually on the same syllable as in the original word.

Examples are:

вор	thief	воришка
го́лос	voice	голоси́шко
го́род	town	городи́шко
дом	house	доми́шко
житьё	life	житьи́шко
забо́р	fence	забо́ришко
заво́д	factory	заво́дишко
запа́с	store	запа́сишко
за́яц	hare	зайчи́шка
здоро́вье	health	здоро́вьишко
купе́ц	merchant	купчи́шка
лгун	liar	лгуни́шка
пальто́	coat	пальти́шко
письмо́	letter	письми́шко
плут	cheat	плути́шка
ружьё	rifle	ружьи́шко
стари́к	old man	старичи́шка (N.B. consonant-change)
челове́к	man	челове́чишка (N.B. consonant-change)

A few diminutives are derived from feminine nouns by means of this suffix:

земля́	land	земли́шка
кварти́ра	flat	кварти́ришка
пого́да	weather	пого́дишка
слу́жба	service	слу́жбишка

(vii)   *The suffix* -ашка

This suffix is used to form diminutives with a slight nuance of disparagement, sometimes endearment. It is non-productive and carries the stress:

ми́лый/-ая	dear	мила́шка
мо́рда, мо́рдочка	muzzle, mug	морда́шка
стари́к	old man	старика́шка

The word промока́шка or промака́шка is slang for 'blotting-paper' (промока́тельная бума́га).

(viii) *The suffix* -онка/-ёнка

This suffix is mainly used in feminine diminutives, occasionally in masculines. It is productive and is associated predominantly with a disparaging, familiar attitude. The stress falls on the suffix:

бáба	woman	бабёнка
бумáга	paper	бумажóнка[1]
избá	hut	избёнка
кни́га	book	книжóнка[1]
корóва	cow	коровёнка
лáвка	shop	лавчóнка[1]
лóшадь	horse	лошадёнка
мáльчик	boy	мальчóнка
		(N.B. omission of ик)
мужи́к	peasant	мужичóнка[1]
погóда	weather	погодёнка
рубáха	shirt	рубашóнка[1]

The word сестрёнка < сестрá 'sister' however is hypocoristic.

c. *Diminutive suffixes of the third degree of expressiveness*

Diminutives of the third degree of expressiveness are those forms which have double diminutive suffixes of the types:

-ечка
    кни́жка   book   кни́жечка
-очка
    вéтка   twig   вéточка
-оночка
    речóнка   stream   речóночка
-урочка
    девчу́рка   little girl   девчу́рочка
-ишечка
    парни́шка   lad   парни́шечка

and so on. As a rule diminutives formed from diminutives have a strongly marked hypocoristic meaning. They are devoid of negative emotional nuances. The meaning of objective diminutiveness is in many cases absent, or is present only to the slightest extent.

The number of diminutives of the third degree of expressiveness is not large, but it can be augmented by including so-called 'author's diminutives', i.e. those which are typical of the individual style of a writer and which serve as a reserve for supplementing the expressive resources of the language.

[1] N.B. consonant-change.

It is interesting to note that only purely Russian words are capable of producing forms with double diminutive suffixes. Words of foreign origin have as a rule only single diminutive forms.

(i) *The suffix* -очка/-ечка

This is used for secondary feminine diminutives formed from diminutives of the first degree of expressiveness with the suffix -ка. The predominant meaning is diminutive-hypocoristic, sometimes only hypocoristic, especially when talking to children. The form -ечка occurs after ш, ж and soft consonants.

The stress falls on the same syllable as in the form with the suffix -ка. This means that in most instances, though not all, the stress falls on the syllable preceding the suffix -очка/-ечка.

This suffix is very productive:

высота́	height	высо́тка	высо́точка
газе́та	newspaper	газе́тка	газе́точка
горсть	handful	го́рстка	го́рсточка
гряда́	bed (in a garden)	гря́дка	гря́дочка
доро́га	way, path	доро́жка[1]	доро́жечка
дочь	daughter	до́чка	до́чечка
ель	fir	ёлка	ёлочка
жи́ла	vein	жи́лка	жи́лочка
ка́ша	porridge	ка́шка	ка́шечка
коро́ва	cow	коро́вка	коро́вочка
котле́та	chop	котле́тка	котле́точка
крова́ть	bed	крова́тка	крова́точка
кроха́	crumb	кро́шка[1]	кро́шечка
ло́шадь	horse	лоша́дка	лоша́дочка
льди́на	ice-floe	льди́нка	льди́ночка
ме́ра	measure	ме́рка	ме́рочка
мину́та	minute	мину́тка	мину́точка
морщи́на	wrinkle	морщи́нка	морщи́ночка
нога́	leg	но́жка[1]	но́жечка
нора́	hole	но́рка	но́рочка
поля́на	glade	поля́нка	поля́ночка
река́	river	ре́чка[1]	ре́чечка
рука́	hand	ру́чка[1]	ру́чечка
сигаре́та	cigarette	сигаре́тка	сигаре́точка
смета́на	sour-cream	смета́нка	смета́ночка
стару́ха	old woman	стару́шка[1]	стару́шечка
тетра́дь	note-book	тетра́дка	тетра́дочка
трава́	grass	тра́вка	тра́вочка
тропа́	path	тро́пка	тро́почка

[1] N.B. consonant-change.

фигу́ра	figure	фигу́рка	фигу́рочка
ха́та	hut	ха́тка	ха́точка
што́ра	blind	што́рка	што́рочка
щепо́ть	pinch	щепо́тка	щепо́точка

Diminutives with the suffix -очка/-ечка are formed also from words in -ка which have lost the diminutive meaning. In these instances, the word from which the diminutive in -очка/-ечка is formed is 'augmented', as it were, i.e. acquires the meaning of relative augmentative. It is doubtless because of the secondary diminutives that the original primary diminutives become independent, i.e. non-diminutive forms:[1]

ви́лка	fork	ви́лочка
голо́вка	head	голо́вочка
гребёнка	comb	гребёночка
дуби́нка	cudgel	дуби́ночка
занаве́ска	curtain	занаве́сочка
иго́лка	needle	иго́лочка
каби́нка	cabin	каби́ночка
карти́нка	illustration	карти́ночка
коло́нка	column, geyser	коло́ночка
корзи́нка	basket	корзи́ночка
ко́рка	crust	ко́рочка
коро́нка	crown	коро́ночка
пе́чка	stove	пе́чечка
пласти́нка	record	пласти́ночка
се́тка	net	се́точка
стре́лка	hand (of a clock)	стре́лочка
ступе́нька	step, rung	ступе́нечка
то́чка	dot	то́чечка
ча́шка	cup	ча́шечка

The degree of expressiveness of diminutives formed from words which have lost their diminutive meaning, especially from words in -ка which are not originally diminutive in meaning (such as гражда́нка, комсомо́лка, игру́шка) is considerably reduced and is in fact first degree, not third degree.

This is even more noticeable in cases when the diminutives with the suffix -очка are formed from substantival roots which end in the consonant clusters—нн, зд, рт, etc.:

ва́нна	bath	ва́нночка
звезда́	star	звёздочка
ка́рта	map	ка́рточка

[1] A few of them may still preserve diminutive meaning (see pp. 16–17).

кофта	woman's jacket	кофточка
кисть	tassel, brush	кисточка
лента	ribbon	ленточка

If such diminutives with the first degree of expressiveness have not already become independent words, they are often well on the way to becoming independent words.

(ii) *The suffix* -ичка

If the suffix -ка is added to a diminutive noun ending in -ица, the ц is changed into ч, giving the double diminutive suffix -ичка, with the stress falling on the same syllable as in the word with the suffix -ица (*q.v.*). This suffix is productive and usually has hypocoristic value:

вещица	thing	вещичка
водица	water	водичка
сестрица	sister	сестричка

This double diminutive suffix should not be confused with the single diminutive suffix -ка added to words ending in -ица or -ика (with change of ц or к to ч) which are not themselves diminutives, such as:

птица	bird	птичка
улица	street	уличка
страница	page	страничка
земляника	wild strawberry	земляничка
клубника	strawberry	клубничка

Nor should it be confused with the non-diminutive suffix -ка, signifying 'female', when this is added to nouns ending in -ик, as in:

большевик	bolshevik	большевичка
меланхолик	melancholic	меланхоличка[1]

(iii) *The suffix* -очек/ёчек

The suffix -очек/-ёчек serves to form masculine diminutives from words which have primary diminutives in -ок/-ёк.[2] The

---

[1] In view of the constant stress (-ичка) in formations of this type, it might be preferable to consider -ичка here as a single suffix. Note also such colloquial forms as электричка 'electric railway' (электрическая железная дорога) or 'electric train'.

[2] There are also a very few diminutives formed with the non-productive suffix -ичек: дождь 'rain'—дождичек, ковш 'ladle'—ковшичек, нож 'knife'—ножичек.

predominant value is hypocoristic. The final vowel is mobile, the suffix has fixed stress on о/ё and is of low productivity:

ветерóк	breeze	ветерóчек
волосóк	hair	волосóчек
голосóк	voice	голосóчек
денёк	day	денёчек
должóк	debt	должóчек
дружóк	friend	дружóчек
дубóк	oak	дубóчек
значóк	badge	значóчек
крючóк	hook	крючóчек
листóк	leaf	листóчек
платóк	handkerchief	платóчек
часóк	hour	часóчек

(iv) *The suffixes* -оночек/-ёночек *and* -оночка/-ёночка

These serve to form double diminutives from primary diminutives with the suffixes -онок/-ёнок and -онка/-ёнка.

The degree of expressiveness of such secondarily formed diminutives is maximal; they have a reinforced hypocoristic value. Such accumulation of diminutive suffixes is, as has already been noted, a specific property of the Slavonic group, in particular of Russian.

The suffixes -оночек/-ёночек, -оночка/-ёночка, all with stress on the first vowel, are productive in modern Russian:

		First degree of expressiveness	Second degree of expressiveness	Third degree of expressiveness
	Original word			
бáба	woman	бáбка	бабёнка	бабёночка
бумáга	paper	бумáжка	бумажóнка	бумажóночка
внук	grandson	внýчек	внучóнок	внучóночек
кнúга	book	кнúжка	книжóнка	книжóночка
козёл	goat	кóзлик	козлёнок	козлёночек
кóмната	room	кóмнатка	комнатёнка	комнатёночка
корóва	cow	корóвка	коровёнка	коровёночка
кот	cat	кóтик	котёнок	котёночек
кóфта	woman's jacket	кóфточка	кофтёнка	кофтёночка
кýкла	doll	кýколка	куклёнка	куклёночка
лóшадь	horse	лошáдка	лошадёнка	лошадёночка
мáльчик	boy	мальчúшка	мальчóнка	мальчóночка
рабóта	work	рабóтка	работёнка	работёночка
рекá	river	рéчка	речóнка	речóночка
рубáха	shirt	рубáшка	рубашóнка	рубашóночка
сестрá	sister	сестрúца	сестрёнка	сестрёночка
старýха	old woman	старýшка	старушóнка	старушóночка
хáта	hut	хáтка	хатёнка	хатёночка

(v) *The suffix* -иночка

This serves to form diminutives of the third degree of expressiveness from diminutives of the first degree of expressiveness which have the suffix -инка. It is productive. The stress is on the same syllable as in the word with the suffix -инка.

The predominant meaning is an extreme degree of diminutiveness with a hypocoristic nuance and, in some instances, singulative meaning:

Original word		*First degree*		*Third degree*
верши́на	top	верши́нка		верши́ночка
кали́на	guelder rose	кали́нка		кали́ночка
кровь	blood	крови́нка	blood particle	крови́ночка
крупа́	groats	крупи́нка	grain, pellet	крупи́ночка
льди́на	ice-floe	льди́нка		льди́ночка
маши́на	machine	маши́нка		маши́ночка
низи́на	low place	низи́нка		низи́ночка
песо́к	sand	песчи́нка	grain of sand	песчи́ночка
полови́на	half	полови́нка		полови́ночка
пух	down	пуши́нка	bit of fluff	пуши́ночка
пыль	dust	пыли́нка	mote of dust	пыли́ночка
середи́на	middle	середи́нка		середи́ночка
снег	snow	снежи́нка	snow flake	снежи́ночка
трава́	grass	трави́нка	blade of grass	трави́ночка
тропа́	path	тропи́нка		тропи́ночка
хворости́на	brush-wood	хворости́нка	switch	хворости́ночка
че́тверть	quarter	четверти́нка		четверти́ночка

(vi) *The suffixes* -ишечка, -ишечко *and* -ушечка/-юшечка

These suffixes, which are of low productivity, form diminutives of the third degree of expressiveness from diminutives of the second degree with the suffixes -ишка, -ишко and -ушка, the stress being on the same syllable as in words with these suffixes (*q.v.*). The suffix -ушечка/-юшечка also forms diminutives of the third degree from diminutives of the second degree with the suffix -уша/-юша. Whereas diminutives of the second stage of expressiveness can have a disparaging meaning, those of the third stage have a clearly expressed meaning of endearment with reinforced expressiveness:

(*a*)

брат	brother	брати́шка	брати́шечка
дом	house	доми́шко	доми́шечко
за́яц	hare	зайчи́шка	зайчи́шечка
ма́льчик	boy	мальчи́шка	мальчи́шечка

40

пальто́	coat	пальти́шко	пальти́шечко
па́рень	lad	парни́шка	парни́шечка
письмо́	letter	письми́шко	письми́шечко

(*b*)

изба́	hut	избу́шка	избу́шечка
ко́мната	room	комнату́шка	комнату́шечка

(*c*)

Илья́	Elias	Илью́ша	Илью́шечка

Note also:

де́вушка	girl	девчу́шка	девчу́шечка
ладо́нь	palm (of hand)	ладо́шка	ладо́шечка

Words in -ушка which have lost their diminutive meaning form diminutives with the suffix -ушечка:

восьму́шка	eight, octavo	восьму́шечка
горбу́шка	crust	горбу́шечка
полу́шка	quarter copeck	полу́шечка
телу́шка	calf	телу́шечка
теплу́шка	heated hut	теплу́шечка

(vii) *The suffixes* -урочка *and* -уленька

These serve to form diminutives, in which the hypocoristic value is strongly marked, from a few first-degree diminutives with the rare and non-productive suffixes -урка and -уля. The stress falls on the vowel y in both suffixes.

		First degree	*Third degree*
де́вочка	girl	девчу́рка	девчу́рочка
до́чка	daughter	дочу́рка	дочу́рочка
ко́шка	cat	кошу́рка	кошу́рочка
пе́чка	stove	печу́рка	печу́рочка
ба́бушка	grandmother	бабу́ля	бабу́ленька
ма́ма	mother	маму́ля	маму́ленька

3

THE FORMATION OF DIMINUTIVE ADJECTIVES

Diminutive forms of qualitative adjectives are formed with the aid of the suffixes:

-енький
| ми́лый | dear | ми́ленький |
| бе́лый | white | бе́ленький |

-онький
| лёгкий | light | лёгонький |
| сухо́й | dry | су́хонький[1] |

-ёхонький
| све́тлый | light | светлёхонький |

-охонький
| лёгкий | light | лего́хонький |

-ошенький
| лёгкий | light | лего́шенький |

-ёшенький
| у́мный | clever | умнёшенький |

-юсенький
| ма́лый/ма́ленький | small | малю́сенький |

-оватый
| кра́сный | red | краснова́тый |

-еватый
| си́ний | blue | синева́тый |

-оватенький
| кра́сный | red | краснова́тенький |

-еватенький
| си́ний | blue | синева́тенький |

Diminutive suffixes impart to the adjective various expressive-emotive nuances, from the meaning of a low degree of the quality:

| хи́трый | хитрова́тый | rather cunning |

to the expression of the emotions of love, tenderness, sympathy and delight:

родно́й	dear, native	ро́дненький
ми́лый	dear	ми́ленький
чу́дный	marvellous	чу́дненький

[1] Also лёгенький, су́хенький.

42

and contempt, hatred, disparagement and disdain:

плохой	bad	плохенький[1]
дешёвый	cheap	дешёвенький
поганый	foul	поганенький

As with the substantival diminutives the meaning of the adjectival diminutive is the result of the interaction of the basic meaning of the original form of the adjective and the emotive-expressive value of the diminutive suffix.

Emotively coloured diminutives from qualitative adjectives are fairly widespread in conversation, in the works of folklore (songs, *byliny*, fairy tales) and also in literature, where they serve as a means of stylization and reinforcement of the expressiveness of speech.

(i) *The suffix* -енький/-онький

This is the most productive of the adjectival diminutive suffixes. Diminutives with this suffix have a wide range of meaning from expressions of positive emotions (love, tenderness, sympathy, compassion) to expressions of negative emotional evaluation (hate, contempt, disparagement, disdain).

The form -онький of this suffix occurs only after к, г and х. Маленький 'small', derived by means of the suffix -енький from the adjective малый, has no particular emotive nuance.

The stress falls on the syllable before the suffix.

The following diminutives with the suffix -енький imply a loving or tender attitude of the speaker to the subject of the conversation:

белый	white	беленький снежок	a little white snowball
бледный	pale	бледненькое личико	a pale little face
гладкий	smooth	гладенький столик	a smooth little table
глупый	stupid	глупенький мальчонка	a silly little boy
голубой	blue	голубенький платочек	a small blue handkerchief
голый	naked	голенький ребёночек	a naked little child
добрый	good, kind	добренький дяденька	a nice uncle
жёлтый	yellow	жёлтенький цветок	a little yellow flower

[1] Also плохонький.

жи́дкий	liquid	жи́денький[1] суп	watery soup
зелёный	green	зелёненькая тра́вка	a small green blade of grass
коро́ткий	short	коро́тенький[1] расска́зик	a very short story
краси́вый	beautiful	краси́венький ви́дик	a lovely view
кра́сный	red	кра́сненький галсту́чек	a red tie
кру́глый	round	кру́гленький ша́рик	a little round ball
ме́лкий	fine, shallow	ме́ленькая[1] ре́чушка	a shallow little stream
ми́лый	dear	ми́ленькая де́вочка	a dear little girl
молодо́й	young	молоде́нький студе́нтик	a nice young student
не́жный	soft, tender	не́жненький голосо́к	a soft voice
ни́зкий	low	ни́зенького[1] ро́ста	small in stature
но́вый	new	но́венький костю́мчик	a new suit
просто́й	simple	про́стенький си́тчик	a simple piece of cotton material
све́жий	fresh	све́женькая газе́тка	a fresh little newspaper
све́тлый	light	све́тленький уголо́к	a nice, bright little corner
се́рый	grey	се́ренький за́йчик	a small grey hare
си́ний	blue	си́ненькая бума́жка	a small piece of blue paper
сла́бый	weak	сла́бенький стари́к	a feeble little old man
сла́вный	glorious	сла́вненький денёчек	a glorious day
сла́дкий	sweet	сла́денький[1] пирожо́к	a small sweet tart
слепо́й	blind	слепе́нький музыка́нт	a small blind musician
сми́рный	quiet	сми́рненькая лоша́дка	a quiet little horse
ста́рый	old	ста́ренький де́душка	a little old grandfather
то́лстый	thick, stout	то́лстенький малы́ш	a fat little child
то́нкий	fine, delicate	то́ненький[1] голосо́к	a thin little voice
тёмный	dark	тёмненькое дельцо́	a shady matter
тяжёлый	heavy	тяжёленький чемода́нчик	a heavy little case
у́зкий	narrow	у́зенькая[1] у́лочка	a narrow little back street
ую́тный	comfortable	ую́тненькая кварти́рка	a comfortable little flat
хи́трый	sly	хи́тренький мальчо́нка	a sly little boy
хоро́ший	fine, beautiful	хоро́шенькая актри́са	a pretty actress
хромо́й	lame	хро́менький мальчуга́н	a little lame boy
худо́й	thin	ху́денькое те́льце	a thin little body
чёрный	black	чёрненькие гла́зки	small black eyes
чи́стый	clean	чи́стенький городо́к	a clean little town

[1] The suffix -кий is omitted when the suffix -енький is added.

Examples of the form -онький, occurring only after к, г or х are:

высо́кая	high	высо́конькая ба́шенка	a high little tower/turret
глубо́кий	deep	глубо́конький коло́дец	a deep little well
лёгкий	light	лёгонький[1] моро́зец	a slight frost
плохо́й	bad	пло́хонькое пальти́шко	a poor little coat
стро́гий	strict	стро́гонький учи́тель	a strict teacher
сухо́й	dry	су́хонький старичо́к	a scraggy little old man
ти́хий	quiet	ти́хонький учени́к	a quiet little pupil
широ́кий	wide	широ́конькая ре́ченька	a wide little stream

(ii) *The suffixes* -ёхонький/-охонький *and* -ёшенький/-ошенький

These serve to form diminutive adjectives with a clearly marked hypocoristic meaning. They are typical of folklore style. In ordinary speech they are rare. The forms in -охонький and -ошенький occur only after к, г and х. The stress falls on the ё/о.

-ёхонький/-охонький:

бли́зкий	близёхонький[2] путь	a very short road
гла́дкий	гладёхонький[2] ка́мешек	a smooth little pebble
жёлтый	желтёхонький цвето́к	a small yellow flower
живо́й	живёхонький верну́лся с фро́нта	He returned alive and kicking from the front
лёгкий	легóхонький толчо́к	a slight nudge
ма́лый	малёхонький ребёночек	a tiny little boy
по́здний	позднёхонький гость	a late guest
по́лный	полнёхонькая корзи́на	an overflowing basket
све́тлый	светлёхонькое не́бо	the bright sky
сми́рный	смирнёхонький телёночек	a gentle little calf

-ёшенький/-ошенький:

бе́лый	белёшенький снежо́к	a little white snowball
здоро́вый	здоровёшенький парни́шка	a healthy young lad
кру́глый	круглёшенький ша́рик	a small round ball
молодо́й	молодёшенький парёнек	a green young lad

Adjectives with the diminutive suffixes -ёхонький and -ёшенький can have short forms:

Отобью́т кусо́к, а у него́, гляди́шь, како́й-нибудь уголо́шек гладёхонек, как зе́ркало блести́т.
(P. Bazhov)

They will break off a piece and he, you see, will have a smooth little corner that will shine like a mirror.

---
[1] The suffix -кий is omitted before the suffix -онький.
[2] The suffix -кий is omitted before the suffix -ёхонький.

...граха éле живёхонька		She was nearly dead [lit. 'barely alive'] with fright.
...молодёшенька была		When I was young

(iii) *The suffix* -юсенький/-усенький

This suffix, which is stressed on the vowel ю/у, serves to form isolated diminutive adjectives with reinforced expression of love and tenderness:

дорогой	дорогусенькая бабусенька	dear little woman
маленький	малюсенький ребёночек	tiny little child
милый	милюсенький мальчоночка	dear little boy
родной	роднюсенький сыночек	dear little son

(iv) *The suffixes* -оватый/-еватый *and* -оватенький/-еватенький

The productive suffix -оватый/-еватый serves to form adjectives expressing the concept of incompleteness of the quality:

белый	white	беловатый	whiteish, slightly white
красный	red	красноватый	reddish, on the red side

In a number of instances adjectives with this suffix express merely incompleteness of the quality without having any emotive-expressive colouring, which leads some linguists not to include them among forms which express a subjective evaluation of the quality expressed (Galkina-Fedoruk, 86). Many diminutives with these suffixes have not lost their expressive meaning, despite the existence of parallel forms in -оватенький/-еватенький with a clearly marked expressive colouring. Hence there are grounds for considering adjectives in -оватый/-еватый to be diminutive forms with some degree or other of expressive colouring, serving to convey the speaker's evaluation of the subject of discourse, especially if the noun qualified is in the diminutive form (cf. холодноватая погодка 'coldish weather', дороговатая книжечка 'a dearish book', плоховатая пьеска 'a poorish play').

The suffix -оватый/-еватый is productive in modern Russian and makes diminutive adjectival forms both from adjectival bases (сладкий 'sweet'—сладковатый) and, less commonly, from substantival bases (плут 'rogue'—плутоватый).

The difference between diminutive forms in -оватый/-еватый and in -оватенький/-еватенький lies in the degree of expressiveness. In the first case we have the minimal degree of expressiveness, in the second (with the addition of a further diminutive suffix) the maximum degree, with the hypocoristic nuance.

In all adjectives formed with these suffixes the stress falls on the vowel a of the suffix.

Forms in -еватый and -еватенький occur only after soft consonants (including ч and щ) and ж, ц and ш:

Original word and meaning		Minimum degree	Example of maximum degree	
бе́лый	white	белова́тый	белова́тенький снежо́к	whiteish snowball
глухо́й	deaf	глухова́тый	глухова́тенькая стару́шка	rather deaf little old woman
голубо́й	blue	голубова́тый	голубова́тенькое пла́тьице	little blue dress
го́рький	bitter	горькова́тый	горькова́тенький грейпфрут	rather bitter grapefruit
гря́зный	dirty	грязнова́тый	грязнова́тенькие ручо́нки	dirty little hands
дорого́й	dear	дорогова́тый	дорогова́тенькая поку́почка	rather dear purchase
жи́дкий	liquid	жидкова́тый	жидкова́тенький суп	watery soup
ки́слый	acid, sour	кислова́тый	кислова́тенький при́вкус	rather sour aftertaste
плохо́й	bad	плохова́тый	плохова́тенькая репута́ция	rather bad reputation
плут	rogue	плутова́тый	плутова́тенький взгляд	roguish glance
ры́жий	sandy-haired	рыжева́тый	рыжева́тенький воротни́к	reddish collar
се́рый	grey	серова́тый	серова́тенький ко́тик	greyish little cat
сла́бый	weak	слабова́тый	слабова́тенький аргуме́нт	weakish argument
ста́рый	old	старова́тый	старова́тенький пиджачи́шко	little old jacket
сухо́й	dry	сухова́тый	сухова́тенький старичо́к	scrawny little old man
твёрдый	firm	твердова́тый	твердова́тенький оре́шек	hard little nut

Examples from literature of the use of diminutive adjectival forms with the suffix -оватый are:

Оста́ток хвоста́ был белесова́тый, пёстрый.　　　　　The stump of his tail was whitish and particoloured.
　　　　　　　(L. Tolstoy)

В её вкусе были блёклые, лиловатые, болотные тона. (А. Tolstoy)	She liked faded, rather lilac, marshy tones.
Мутноватые стёкла, почернелая позолота рам... (К. Paustovski)	The dull panes, the blackened gilding of the frames...
В его глазах временами вспыхивали хитроватые, лукавые огоньки. (М. Alekseyev)	Rather cunning, sly little flashes would sparkle in his eyes from time to time.
Дитя же растёт криво ватым. (*Literaturnaya gazeta*)	The child is growing up rather twisted.

It is clear from the examples given that the suffix -оватый is productive in modern Russian and conveys various shades of meaning, expressing the attitude of the speaker, even if only to a weak degree.[1]

The expressive-emotive suffix -оватенький/-еватенький is to be met with in conversational speech, but is not typical of the literary style. The possibility of forming diminutives in -оватенький/-еватенький may rather be described as potential: these are the diminutives which are to be found on the fringe of the creative possibilities of Russian.

On the whole diminutives from adjectives occur more frequently in Russian than in English. It is likely that English speakers, being more reserved in their expression of emotion, try to avoid the two extremes of language—on the one hand the widespread use of the superlative, and on the other the use of descriptive diminutives—while in spoken Russian the converse is to be observed.

---

[1] Adjectives with the suffix -оватый/-еватый can be found in the comparative degree, e.g.:

белый	white	беловатее	more whiteish
слабый	weak	слабоватее	rather weaker, more on the weak side
сухой	dry	суховатее	more dryish

and so on.

Diminutive forms with other suffixes (беленький, слабенький, сухонький) do not form comparatives.

4

DIMINUTIVE FORMS OF ADVERBS

In addition to diminutives of nouns and adjectives, there are also diminutive forms of adverbs, occurring both in conversational and literary Russian:

немно́го	little, a little	немно́жко
осторо́жно	careful	осторо́жненько
тру́дно	with difficulty	трудновáто

and so on.

Adverbs with the diminutive suffixes -енько (-онько[1]), -енечко (-онечко[1]), -ехонько (-охонько[1]), -ешенько (-ошенько[1]), -ко, -ечко, -овато/-евато, take on the additional meanings of intensification or attenuation of the adverbial quality or have hypocoristic value.

Diminutive adverbs with the suffix -енько/-онько form the largest group. They are used to render the additional expressive colouring of an increase or a decrease in the adverbial quality (depending on the basic meaning of the adverb itself). As a rule the expressive-emotive nuances of diminutive adverbs are supported by a reinforcement of the phrasal (emphatic) accent:

Она́ живёт совсе́м бли́зенько [< бли́зко]	She lives quite near
Да́вненько мы с ва́ми не ви́делись (familiar-condescending tone)	It's a long time since we saw you
До́лгонько вы отсу́тствовали (intensified and condescending)	You've been away a long time
Краси́венько всё э́то вы́глядит (ironic)	How beautiful it all looks
Я люблю́ тебя́ кре́пенько[2]	I love you so much (lit. 'strongly')
Она́ легóнько[2] толкну́ла его́	She gave him a slight nudge
Жил бы хороше́нько, да де́нег мале́нько	He would live well, but he has little money
Мно́гонько у него́ добра́ (implying 'quite enough')	He has plenty/He lacks for nothing (lit. 'He has plenty of goods/property')

[1] After г, к and х.
[2] Note the omission of the suffix -ко of the basic form (кре́пко, легкó).

Он не́жненько поцелова́л её	He tenderly kissed her
По́здненько вы пришли́ (ironic)	You are a little bit late
Вста́нешь ра́ненько, всё сде́лать успе́ешь (intensification)	If you get up early, you will manage to get everything done
Сиди́ сми́рненько	Sit still
Отвеча́ет ему спокойненько (ironic)	He answers him quietly
Тру́дненько вам пришло́сь	You've had a hard time of it
Холо́дненько тут у вас	Your place (house/apartment) is a bit on the cold side
Запо́мните э́то хороше́нько (intensified meaning)	Make sure and remember this (lit. 'Remember this well')
Он ча́стенько тут быва́л (possibly with an ironic undertone)	He was here quite often

Diminutive adverbs in -енько/-онько show some vacillation in the position of the stress. Some of them are given in dictionaries with alternative stress, e.g.:

бы́стренько/быстре́нько	(< бы́стро)	quickly
ки́сленько/кисле́нько	(< ки́сло)	bitterly
ла́дненько/ладне́нько	(< ла́дно)	well, in harmony
не́жненько/нежне́нько	(< не́жно)	tenderly
ни́зенько/низе́нько[1]	(< ни́зко)	low

[1] In this connection the author of a recent article dealing with diminutive adverbs (Ivanova) puts forward the suggestion that in modern Russian 'the following relationship is being formed: if the stress falls on the suffix, then the suffix usually adds to the meaning a nuance of incompleteness of the quality —"fairly", "to some extent",' thus:

высоко́нько	fairly high
давне́нько	fairly long ago
холодне́нько	rather cold
часте́нько	fairly often

and so on.

'If the stress falls on the stem, then the suffix acquires the meaning of "subjectively coloured intensification or reinforcement"; it adds as it were the meaning of "quite/altogether" or "very"':

бли́зенько = совсе́м, о́чень бли́зко	quite/very near
бы́стренько = совсе́м/о́чень бы́стро	quite/very fast
ни́зенько = совсе́м/о́чень ни́зко	quite/very low
то́ненько = совсе́м/о́чень то́нко	quite/very finely/delicately

and so on.

'Thus the position of the stress influences to some extent the meaning of the adverb, giving additional shades of meaning to the original one.'

The following, further examples of diminutive adverbs in -енько/-онько are taken from literary works:

— И чего́ ты не пришибёшь его́, Васи́лий?	And why don't you do him in, Vasily?
— Ста́ну я и́з-за вся́кой дря́ни кровь себе́ по́ртить.	Expect me to get worked up for every piddling thing?
— А ты у́мненько. (M. Gorky)	You're acting smart then
О́коло сане́й лего́нько бежа́л молодо́й мужи́к. (A. Bunin)	A young peasant ran nimbly along beside the sledge
Да́ша, разде́вшись в свое́й чи́стенько при́бранной ко́мнатке... (A. Tolstoy)	Dasha, having undressed in her room, now neatly tidied...
Кри́тику осторо́жненько должно́ вести́. (Mayakovsky)	Criticism should be made with care
А та ничего́, стои́т споко́йненько. (P. Bazhov)	And she does nothing, just stands quietly there
Лишь бы ры́жим не звала́, да поласко́венько погляде́ла. (P. Bazhov)	If only she didn't call him ginger and would look at him tenderly

The suffixes -енечко/-онечко, -ехонько/-охонько, -ешенько are used to form diminutive adverbs with hypocoristic meaning:

Она́ лего́нечко посту́кивала па́льцами по́ столу	She tapped lightly on the table with her fingers
Я мале́нечко опозда́л	I am just a little late
Наро́ду собрало́сь полны́м-полнёхонько	There gathered together a whole lot of people
Иди́, сыно́к, прямёхонько че́рез по́ле	Go, son, straight across the field
Ранёхонько ты встала, до́ченька!	You've got up early, daughter
Он, тихо́нечко, на цы́почках прошёл ми́мо две́ри.	He slipped quietly past the door on tiptoes
А звёздочки тонёхонько позва́нивают. (P. Bazhov)	And the little stars delicately tinkle

The suffixes -ко, -ечко, -овато/-евато form diminutive adverbs with additional subjective colouring (sometimes with intensifying function):

Костю́м немно́жко/немно́жечко коротко́ват	The suit is rather on the short side

Глухова́то прозвуча́л вы́стрел	The shot rang out dully
Э́то для меня́ дорогова́то	That is rather dear for me
Малова́то оста́лось де́нег	There was very little money left
Плохова́то он игра́л сего́дня	He played rather badly today
У меня́ сухова́то во рту	My mouth's rather dry
В лесу́ бы́ло сырова́то	It was rather damp in the wood
В ко́мнате бы́ло темнова́то	The room was pretty dark
Труднова́то бы́ло ей жить одно́й	She found it rather hard to live alone
Ве́чером на у́лице бы́ло холоднова́то	In the evening the street was rather cold

Diminutive-forming suffixes are to be observed in the adverbs illustrated below. These adverbs are 'colloquial' (though this does not mean that they do not occur in literature) and often have expressive colouring:

Он бочко́м продви́нулся ме́жду ряда́ми кре́сел. (cf. бо́ком)[1]	He edged himself sideways between the rows of seats
Дом располо́жен наискосо́к от шоссе́. (cf. на́искось)	The house was sited obliquely to the highway
Он понемно́жку выздора́вливал по́сле тяжёлой боле́зни. (cf. понемно́гу)	He was gradually recovering after a serious illness
Кот потихо́ньку пробра́лся в чула́н.[2] (cf. ти́хо)	The cat made its way noiselessly into the storeroom
Она́ укра́дочкой поцелова́ла его́. (cf. укра́дкой)	She gave him a furtive kiss

5

THE QUESTION OF VERBAL DIMINUTIVES

Diminutive verbs are a very rare phenomenon in the Indo-European languages. Even in those languages rich in diminutives, such as the Baltic group, only isolated instances of diminutives from verbs are to be found, mainly in the speech of children and in conversation with children.

[1] Бочко́м may have the additional implication of timidity or deference.
[2] See also example no. 3 on p. 54.

Verbal diminutives are to be found too in the Slavic languages, for instance in Ukrainian and White Russian, which are closely related to Russian. Even in these languages, however, the choice of verbs lending themselves to diminutivization is also very limited. They are the verbs 'to eat', 'to drink' and 'to sleep'. Here is an example from a Ukrainian wedding song, where the diminutive verbs are used in the infinitive with a hypocoristic nuance:

Не хочу я *їстоньки* та *питоньки*	I don't want to eat or to drink
Бо вже моє тіло *спатоньки* схотіло	For my body already wants to sleep
(їстоньки < їсти	to eat
питоньки < пити	to drink
спатоньки < спати	to sleep)

The diminutive-hypocoristic verb спатки/спаточки/спатоньки is found in colloquial Russian in conversation with children. Purely diminutive verbal forms, however, are not typical of Russian. Nevertheless, it seems that, apart from their basic meaning, some verbal forms have, in certain contexts the subjectively coloured nuances of diminutiveness (a diminution of the action), analogous to the nuances expressed by diminutive suffixes in substantival, adjectival and adverbial diminutives.

Let us consider a few examples:

1. Он, знай, похохáтывает. He just chuckles away to himself
   (P. Bazhov)

The choice of the imperfective похохáтывать (formed from хохотáть 'to laugh' with the prefix по- and the suffix -ыва-) is to be explained, it would seem, by the author's desire to render the subjective-expressive nuance of diminution of the action, together with the implication '...he doesn't care...he knows what it's all about, but he only chuckles...'. Apart from this, the given verb form fits the general style of the narrative, which is full of diminutives from other parts of speech.

2. Пощи́пывая ре́дкую боро́дку, Plucking at his sparse beard, Akundin
   Акýндин оглядéл затúхший зал. looked round the silent room
   (A. Tolstoy)

We have the same verbal model as in the previous example (пощи́пывать < щипáть 'to pinch'), with the meaning of reduced action (not merely pinching from time to time, but gently plucking at the beard). Here, however, the use of a verb form with a diminutive nuance accords with the diminutive form of the object of the action (боро́дка < борода́ 'beard').

3. Она́ обняла́ нас за пле́чи и, прихра́мывая, а иногда́ совсе́м поджима́я но́гу, начала́ потихо́нечку спуска́ться по шоссе́. (K. Paustovsky)	Putting her arms round our shoulders, limping slightly and at times keeping her foot off the ground altogether, she began gingerly to make her way down the road

The verb прихра́мывать ('to limp slightly') from хрома́ть ('to limp') has the meaning of reduced action. Characteristic is the presence of the diminutive adverb потихо́нечку ('gently', 'slowly').

4. Тут и парти́йными взыска́ниями попа́хивает. (A. Arbuzov)	There's a faint suggestion [lit. 'whiff, smell'] of party reprimand about it too[1]

The verb form попа́хивает from па́хнуть ('to smell') is used in the given case to render, beside the basic meaning, the additional nuance of diminished action—not a 'smell' but merely a 'whiff'.

5. Двух пере́дних зубо́в у неё не́ было, говори́ла она́ пришепётывая... (*Izvestiya*)	She had lost her two front teeth and spoke with a slight lisp

The verb пришепётывать from шепета́ть (now rare) has, in the given case, not only the meaning of diminished action, but also, as becomes clear from the general content of the story, a certain psychological undertone—it expresses the benevolent attitude of the author to the heroine. The author strives, by minimizing her physical defect, to arouse the reader's sympathy and thus dispose him kindly towards her.

 The examples given lead to the suggestion that some Russian verbs (with the prefixes по-, при- and the suffix -ыва-/-ива-) have the capacity of expressing, in addition to their basic meaning, the diminutive nuance of reduced action with some subjective expressive colouring or other.

 It is interesting to note that all these verbs are imperfective and that they do not have parallel perfective forms. In the literature on this subject (in the Academy grammar, for instance) there are indications that the meaning of non-paired imperfective verbs with the prefixes по- and при- and the suffixes -ова—and -ива—

---

[1] Example suggested by D. Ward.

do not fit into the existing classification, according to which they are treated as verbs with iterative meaning.

This question is touched on by Ward (227-8), who quite rightly objects to the inclusion of such verbs as помáргивать ('to blink'), поплёвывать ('to spit'), попáхивать ('to smell'), прихрáмывать ('to limp'), in the category of iteratives, and points to the fact that in the Russian verbal aspect system certain shifts are to be noted. To take this idea further, we may suggest that one of the results of this process may be the appearance and further development of the diminutive-expressive nuances in non-paired imperfective verbs with the prefixes по-, при- and the suffix -ыва-/-ива-.[1]

Definitive conclusions on the question of verbal diminutives can of course only be arrived at after special research based on extensive material both from the spoken and the literary language.

6

CONCLUSIONS

1. Diminutivization is one of the most important expressive resources in Russian. With the aid of diminutives Russian can render various shades of expressiveness and subjective colouring: tenderness, affection, delight, friendly attitude, irony, scorn, contempt, flattery, condescension and familiarity. In the majority of cases the diminutive-hypocoristic meaning is dominant.

2. In modern Russian, in connection with the development of expressive resources, a tendency towards the more widespread use of diminutive forms is to be noted. From the conversational style, diminutives spread more and more into literature and there they are used not merely as a means of stylization or linguistic

---

[1] There are verbs with the prefix под- which have the meaning 'performance of the action to a limited degree' such as подмерзáть, подмёрзнуть 'to freeze slightly'; подсыхáть, подсóхнуть 'to get a little bit drier'; подсýшивать, подсушúть 'to dry a little'; поджáривать, поджáрить 'to brown'; etc. These too might be classified as 'diminutive verbs'. The process of formation of such verbs appears to be productive — Онá мне за э́тот вéчер порядком поднадоéла. (V. Voinovich) 'She bored me pretty well stiff that evening.'

characterization of the dramatis personae, but also in the author's own words.

3. Russian is rich in suffixes for creating diminutives. To form diminutives from nouns more than thirty suffixes may be used; there is also a whole series to form diminutives from adjectives and adverbs. The possiblity of forming a limited number of verbal diminutives is not excluded.

4. Depending on the interaction of the meaning of the basic word and that of the diminutive suffix, three degrees of expressiveness may be distinguished. Moreover, the degree of diminutiveness is affected by such factors as the range of use, the context, the intonation and also the mood of the speaker and his ability to use these means of subjective colouring.

5. Within the system of Russian diminutives a constant process of development is taking place: some diminutives become independent words, adding to and enriching the lexical stock of the language, others branch out into diminutive series which can render the most delicate nuances and gradations of expressiveness.

6. Students of Russian who want to master the spoken language and be able to read Russian literature with complete understanding of the emotive-expressive undertones, should pay particular attention to the study of diminutives. Once having mastered this expressive resource they will be able to understand and appreciate properly the beauty and expressiveness of the Russian language.

APPENDICES

1. *Alphabetical list of diminutive noun suffixes*

The following list sums up the salient information given in the body of the book on diminutive noun suffixes and also serves as an index. The suffixes are listed alphabetically, their degree of expressiveness and productivity[1] is indicated and the relevant section of chapter 2, with page number, is given.

Suffix	Degree of expressiveness	Degree of productivity	Section of chapter 2 and page
-ашка	2	non-productive	B, vii, 34
-ёк, see -ок/-ёк			
-ёнка, see -онка/-ёнка			
-ёнок/-онок	1	productive	A, vii, 27
-ёночек, see -оночек/-ёночек			

[1] On degrees of productivity see Ward (112).

Suffix	Degree of expressiveness	Degree of productivity	Section of chapter 2 and page
-ёночка, see -оночка/-ёночка			
-ёныш	1	very low productivity	A, vii, 27
-енька	2	productive	B, i, 30
-ец	1	low productivity	A, vi, 26
-(е)цо/-(и)це	1	very low productivity	A, v, 24
-ёчек, see -очек/-ёчек			
-ечка, see -очка/-ечка			
-ик	1	productive	A, ii, 18
-ико, see -ко			
-инка	1	productive	A, ix, 28
-иночка	3	productive	C, v, 40
-ица	1	non-productive	A, viii, 28
-(и)це, see -(е)цо/-(и)це			
-ичка	3	productive	C, ii, 38
-ишечка	3	low productivity	C, vi, 40
-ишечко	3	low productivity	C, vi, 40
-ишка	2	fairly productive	B, vi, 33
-ишко	2	fairly productive	B, vi, 33
-ка	1	very productive	A, i, 13
-ко	1	non-productive	A, xi, 29
-ок/-ёк	1	low productivity	A, iv, 22
-онка/-ёнка	2	productive	B, viii, 35
-онок, see -ёнок/-онок			
-оночек/-ёночек	3	productive	C, iv, 39
-оночка/-ёночка	3	productive	C, iv, 39
-онька	2	productive	B, ii, 31
-очек/-ёчек	3	low productivity	C, iii, 38
-очка/-ечка	3	productive	C, i, 36
-уленька	3	non-productive	C, vii, 41
-урочка	3	non-productive	C, vii, 41
-уша/-юша	2	non-productive	B, iv, 33
-ушечка/-юшечка	3	low productivity	C, vi, 40
-ушка/-юшка	2	fairly productive	B, iii, 32
-ушко/-юшко	2	non-productive	B, iii, 32
-ца	1	non-productive	A, xii, 30
-це, see -(е)цо/-(и)це			
-цо, see -(е)цо/-(и)це			
-чик	1	productive	A, iii, 21
-ыш	1	non-productive	A, x, 29
-ышек	2	non-productive	B, v, 33
-ышко	2	low productivity	B, v, 33
-юша, see -уша/-юша			
-юшечка, see -ушечка/-юшечка			
-юшка, see -ушка/-юшка			
-юшко, see -ушко/-юшко			

2. *Grammatical and phonetic notes*

(a) Gender

Feminine diminutives are by far the most numerous, especially with suffixes of reinforced expressiveness. In the vast majority of cases diminutives keep the grammatical gender of the original word:

вещь	thing	вещи́ца
вода́	water	води́ца
гнездо́	nest	гнёздышко
друг	friend	дружо́к
зе́ркало	mirror	зе́ркальце
зима́	winter	зиму́шка
рука́	hand	ру́чка

Instances of change of grammatical gender in the formation of diminutives are relatively few in number:

ве́чер	evening	вечери́нка	party
песо́к	sand	песчи́нка	grain of sand
пух	down	пуши́нка	bit of fluff
сор	litter	сори́нка	mote

etc.

Note that diminutives denoting male beings keep the masculine gender, even when the diminutive suffix ends in -a: стари́к — старика́шка 'old man'; дя́дя — дя́денька 'uncle'; Па́вел — Павлу́ша 'Paul'; etc. The same applies to diminutives formed from masculine nouns by means of the suffix -ишко, thus доми́шко (< дом) 'small house' is masculine.

Thus the diminutive suffixes used in forming nouns may be classified according to gender and degree of expressiveness as follows:

Masculine

First degree of expressiveness: -ик, -чик, -ок/-ёк, -ец, -ёнок/-онок, -ёныш, -ыш;

Second: -енька, -онька, -ушка/-юшка, -уша/-юша, -ышек, -ишко, -ишка, -ашка and -онка/-ёнка;

Third: -очек/-ёчек, -оночек/-ёночек, and -ишечка, -ишечко, -ушечка/-юшечка.

Feminine

First degree of expressiveness: -ка, -ица, -инка, -ца;

Second: -енька, -онька, -ушка/-юшка, -уша/-юша, -ишка, -ашка, -онка/-ёнка;

Third: -очка/-ечка, -ичка, -оночка/-ёночка, -иночка, -ишечка, -ушечка/-юшечка, -урочка, -уленька.

Neuter

First degree of expressiveness: -(е)цо/-(и)це, -ко, -ико;
Second: -ушко/-юшко, -ышко, -ишко;
Third: -ишечко.

(b) Stress

Diminutive noun-suffixes are classified below according to the position of the stress. In each section the suffixes are listed alphabetically, according to the first letter of the suffix.

1. *Suffixes which always carry stress:*
    -а́шка
    -ёнок/-о́нок
    -ёныш
    -и́нка, -и́ночка (some exceptions)
    -о́к/-ёк (shifting to endings in oblique cases)
    -о́нка/-ёнка
    -о́ночек/-ёночек
    -о́ночка/-ёночка
    -о́чек/-ёчек
    -у́ля and -у́ленька
    -у́рка and -у́рочка
    -у́ша/-ю́ша
    -ца́ (strictly speaking, endings are stressed)

2. *Suffixes with which the stress always falls on the stem:*
    (a) on the syllable before the suffix:
        -енька
        -онька
        -ушка/-юшка, -ушечка/-юшечка, -ушко/-юшко (usually), -ышко and -ышек
    (b) as in original noun:
        -ик
        -чик

3. *Variable:*
    -ец: if the original noun has stress-shift, then -е́ц, with stress shifting to endings in oblique cases; otherwise as in original noun.
    -(е)цо/-(и)це: if the original noun is stressed on the stem, then so is the diminutive; otherwise -(е)цо́.
    -ико: as -ко.
    -ица: if the original noun ends in -ь or stressed -а́/-я́ in the nom. sg., then -и́ца; otherwise as in original noun.
    -ичка: as -ица.
    -ишечка/-ишечко: as -ишко and -ишка.
    -ишко and -ишка: if the original noun has stress on the endings or shifting on to the endings, then -и́шко, -и́шка; otherwise usually as in original noun.
    -ка: if the original word is a derived word, then the stress is as in the original word; otherwise on the root-syllable (see p. 14).
    -ко and -ико: unpredictable.
    -очка/-ечка: as -ка.
    -ыш: if the original word has final stress in any of its forms, then -ы́ш, with stress shifting to endings in oblique cases; otherwise as in original word.

(c) Consonant alternations

Diminutive noun suffixes beginning with the letters е, е/о or и require the following consonant changes to take place:

$$\text{г} > \text{ж}$$
$$\text{к} > \text{ч}$$
$$\text{х} > \text{ш}$$
$$\text{ц} > \text{ч}$$

Suffixes beginning with е/о then take the alternative spelling with о if stressed.

Examples are:

г > ж:

долг	debt	должо́к, должо́чек
друг	friend	дружо́к, дружо́чек
бума́га	paper	бума́жонка
кни́га	book	кни́жка, кни́жечка, книжо́нка, книжо́ночка
снег	snow	снежи́нка, снежи́ночка ('snow-flake')
доро́га	road	доро́женька[1]

к > ч

крюк	hook	крючо́к
рука́	hand	ру́чка, ру́ченька
песо́к	sand	песчи́нка ('grain of sand')
соба́ка	dog	соба́чка, собачо́нка
внук	grandson	внучо́нок, внучо́ночек
река́	river	ре́чка, речо́ночка
стари́к	old man	старичи́шка

х > ш

пух	down	пушо́к, пуши́нка ('mote', 'fluff')
пасту́х	shepherd	пастушо́к
стару́ха	old woman	старушо́нка
стих	verse	стишо́к

ц > ч

лицо́	face	ли́чико
коне́ц	end	ко́нчик ('tip')
огуре́ц	gherkin	огу́рчик

The suffixes -ка, -ушка and -ушечка produce the same effect, as in
река́   river   ре́чка, ре́чушка, речу́шечка.

3. *Lexical sets of diminutives*

Some common nouns, arranged in lexical sets, are given below with some of their diminutives. The three degrees of expressiveness are indicated by the figures 1, 2 and 3, preceded by one or more of the abbreviations shown on p. 61, indicating the particular nuance of each word:[2]

---

[1] Note also медве́дь 'bear', медвежо́нок 'bear-cub'.

[2] These nuances are either generally accepted or such as they were interpreted by the author in particular contexts (Ed.).

comp.	compassionate
cond.	condescending
cont.	contemptuous
dim.	diminutive
dim.-hyp.	diminutive-hypocoristic
disp.	disparaging
fam.	familiar
hyp.	hypocoristic
ingrat.	ingratiating
iron.	ironic
neutr.	neutral

Relationships

брат 'brother', брáтец (iron., fam. 1), братишка (fam. 2)
дед 'grandfather', дедóк (iron., fam. 1), дéдушка (hyp. 2), дедýся (hyp. 3)
дочь 'daughter', дóчка (neut., fam. or scorn. 1), дóченька (hyp. 2), дочýрочка (hyp. 3)
дя́дя 'uncle', дя́дька (disp. 1), дя́денька (hyp. 2), дя́дечка (hyp. 3)
жених 'bridegroom', женишóк (iron. 1)
зять 'son-in-law', зятёк (iron. 1)
мáма 'mother', мáменька (hyp. 2), мáмочка (hyp. 3), мамýленька (hyp. 3)
муж 'husband', муженёк (iron., hyp. 1)
невéста 'bride', невéстушка (hyp. 2)
невéстка 'daughter-in-law', невéсточка (hyp. 2)
пáпа 'father', пáпенька (hyp. 2), пáпочка (hyp. 3), папýленька (hyp. 3)
племя́нник 'nephew', племя́нничек (hyp. 1)
семья́ 'family', семéйка (iron. 1)
сестрá 'sister', сестрица (hyp. 1), сестрёнка (hyp. 2), сестричка (dim.-hyp. 3), сестрёночка (dim.-hyp. 3)
сын 'son', сынóк (hyp. 1), сынóчек (hyp. 3), сынýленька (hyp. 3)
тётя 'aunt', тётка (disp. 1), тётенька (hyp. 2), тётушка (hyp. 2), тётечка (hyp. 3)

Parts of the body

бок 'side', бочóк (dim.-hyp. 1)
бородá 'beard', борóдка (dim. 1), борóдушка (hyp. 2), бородёнка (disp. 2)
вóлосы 'hair', волóсики (hyp. 1), волосёнки (dim.-hyp. 2)
глазá 'eyes', глáзки (hyp. 1)
головá 'head', голóвка (dim.-hyp. 1), голóвушка (hyp. 2), головёнка (dim.-hyp. 2)
гýбы 'lips', гýбки (hyp. 1)
живóт 'belly', живóтик (dim.-hyp. 1)
жила 'vein', жилка (dim. 1), жилочка (dim.-hyp. 3)
зуб 'tooth', зýбик (dim.-hyp. 1), зубóк (dim.-hyp. 1)
кóжа 'skin', кóжица (dim. 1)
кость 'bone', кóсточка (dim. 3)
кулáк 'fist', кулачóк (dim. 1), кулачóчек (hyp. 3)
ладóнь 'palm', ладóшка (dim.-hyp. 2)
лицó 'face', личико (dim.-hyp. 1)

лоб 'forehead', лобик (dim.-hyp. 1)
локоть 'elbow', локоток (dim.-hyp. 1)
ноготь 'fingernail', ноготок (dim.-hyp. 1)
нос 'nose', носик (dim.-hyp. 1)
палец 'finger', пальчик (dim.-hyp. 1)
плечо 'shoulder', плечико (dim.-hyp. 1)
подбородок 'chin', подбородочек (dim.-hyp. 1)
рот 'mouth', ротик (dim.-hyp. 1)
рука 'hand', ручка (dim.-hyp. 1), рученька (hyp. 2), ручонка (dim.-hyp. 2), ручоночка (dim.-hyp. 3)
сердце 'heart', сердечко (dim.-hyp. 1)
спина 'back', спинка (dim.-hyp. 1)
тело 'body', тельце (dim.-hyp. 1)
темя 'temple', темечко (dim.-hyp. 3)
ухо 'ear', ушко (hyp. 1)
фигура 'figure', фигурка (hyp. 1), фигурочка (hyp. 3)
шея 'neck', шейка (hyp. 1)
щека 'cheek', щёчка (hyp. 1)
язык 'tongue', язычок (hyp. 1)

Dress and footwear
бельё 'linen', бельецо (dim.-hyp. 1)
ботинки 'shoes', ботиночки (dim.-hyp. 1)
брюки 'trousers', брючки (dim.-hyp. 1)
воротник 'collar', воротничок (dim. 1)
галстук 'tie', галстучек (dim. 1)
джемпер 'jumper', джемперок (dim. 1), джемперочек (dim.-hyp. 3)
каблук 'heel', каблучок (dim. 1)
карман 'pocket', карманчик (dim. 1)
кепка 'cap', кепочка (hyp. 1)
кофта '(woman's) jacket', кофтёнка (disp. 2), кофточка (dim.-hyp. 3)
костюм 'suit', костюмчик (hyp. 1), костюмишко (disp. 2)
куртка 'short jacket', курточка (dim.-hyp. 1)
носки 'socks', носочки (dim. 1)
одежда 'clothes', 'dress', одежонка (disp. 2)
пиджак 'jacket', пиджачок (dim.-hyp. 1), пиджачишко (disp. 2)
пижама 'pyjamas', пижамка (dim. 1), пижамочка (hyp. 3)
платок 'handkerchief', платочек (dim.-hyp. 1)
платье 'dress', платьице (dim.-hyp. 1)
пояс 'belt', поясок (dim.-hyp. 1)
рубашка 'shirt', рубашечка (dim.-hyp. 1)
сапоги 'boots', сапожки (dim.-hyp. 1), сапожочки (hyp. 3)
сарафан 'sarafan', сарафанчик (hyp. 1)
свитер 'sweater', свитерок (dim.-hyp. 1)
трусы 'shorts', трусики (dim. 1)
туфли 'shoes', 'slippers', туфельки (dim.-hyp. 1), туфлишки (disp. 2)
халат 'dressing-gown', халатик (dim.-hyp. 1), халатишко (disp. 2)
чулки 'stockings', чулочки (dim.-hyp. 1)
шапка 'cap', шапочка (dim.-hyp. 1)
шарф 'scarf', шарфик (dim.-hyp. 1)

шля́па 'hat', шля́пка (dim.-hyp. 1), шля́почка (hyp. 3)
шу́ба 'fur-coat', шу́бка (dim.-hyp. 1), шу́бочка (hyp. 3), шубе́йка (disp. 2)
ю́бка 'skirt', ю́бочка (dim.-hyp. 1), юбчо́нка (disp. 2)

Food and drink

апельси́н 'orange', апельси́нчик (dim.-hyp. 1)
арбу́з 'melon', арбу́зик (dim.-hyp. 1), арбу́зишко (disp. 2)
борщ 'borsch', борщо́к (hyp. 1), бо́рщец (hyp., fam. 1)
вино́ 'wine', винцо́ (hyp., fam. 1), вини́шко (disp. 2)
во́дка 'vodka', во́дочка (hyp., fam. 1)
говя́дина 'beef', говя́динка (hyp. 1)
жир 'fat', жиро́к (hyp. 1), жиро́чек (hyp., fam. 3)
изю́м 'raisin', изю́мчик (hyp. 1)
икра́ 'caviare', ико́рка (hyp. 1)
ка́ша 'porridge', ка́шка (hyp. 1), ка́шица (hyp. 1)
кисе́ль '*kisel*', 'compote', киселёк (hyp. 1)
колбаса́ 'sausage', колба́ска (hyp. 1), колба́сочка (hyp. 3)
конфе́та 'sweet', конфе́тка (hyp. 1), конфе́точка (hyp. 3)
коньа́к 'cognac', коньячо́к (hyp., fam. 1)
котле́та 'chop', котле́тка (hyp. 1), котле́точка (hyp. 3)
ко́фе 'coffee', кофеёк (hyp. 1), кофеёчек (hyp. 3)
лапша́ 'noodles', лапши́ца (hyp. 1)
лимо́н 'lemon', лимо́нчик (hyp. 1)
лук 'onion', лучо́к (dim.-hyp. 1)
ма́сло 'butter', ма́слице (hyp. 1)
мёд 'honey', медо́к (hyp. 1)
молоко́ 'milk', молочко́ (hyp. 1), молочи́шко (disp. 2)
морко́вь 'carrot', морко́вка (dim. 1), морко́вочка (dim.-hyp. 3)
мука́ 'flour', му́чка (hyp. 1), му́чица (hyp., fam. 1)
мя́со 'meat', мясцо́ (hyp. 1)
огуре́ц 'cucumber', огу́рчик (hyp. 1)
пе́нка 'skin (on milk, etc.)', пе́ночка (hyp. 1)
пе́рец 'pepper', пе́рчик (hyp. 1)
пече́нье 'biscuit', пече́ньице (hyp. 1)
пи́во 'beer', пивцо́ (hyp., fam. 1)
пшени́ца 'wheat', пшени́чка (hyp. 1)
са́ло 'dripping', са́льце (hyp. 1)
са́хар 'sugar', сахаро́к (hyp. 1)
смета́на 'sour cream', смета́нка (hyp. 1)
соси́ска 'sausage', соси́сочка (hyp. 1)
суп 'soup', су́пик (hyp. 1), су́пчик (hyp. 1), супи́шко (disp. 2)
суха́рь 'rusk', суха́рик (dim.-hyp. 1)
сыр 'cheese', сыро́к (hyp. 1), сыро́чек (hyp. 3)
творо́г 'curds', творожо́к (hyp. 1), творожо́чек (hyp. 3)
теля́тина 'veal', теля́тинка (hyp. 1)
торт 'cake', то́ртик (hyp. 1), то́ртишко (disp. 2)
хлеб 'bread', хлебе́ц (fam. 1), хле́бушко (hyp. 2)
хрен 'horse-radish', хрено́к (hyp., fam. 1)
чай 'tea', чаёк (hyp. 1), чайшко (disp. 2)
шокола́д 'chocolate', шокола́дик (hyp. 1)

щи 'cabbage soup', щец[1] (hyp., fam. 1)
яблоко 'apple', яблочко (dim.-hyp. 1)

Animals

ёж 'hedgehog', ёжик (dim. 1), ежо́нок (dim. 1), ежо́ночек (hyp. 3)
жеребёнок 'foal', жеребёночек (dim.-hyp. 3)
за́яц 'hare', за́йчик (dim. 1), зайчи́шка (fam. 1), зайчо́нок (dim. 1), зайчо́ночек (dim.-hyp. 3)
зверь 'animal', зверёк (dim. 1), зверёныш (dim. 1), зве́рушка (hyp. 2)
змея́ 'snake', зме́йка (dim. 1), змее́чка (hyp. 3)
канаре́йка 'canary', канаре́ечка (dim.-hyp. 1), канаре́юшка (hyp. 2)
коза́ 'goat', ко́зочка (dim.-hyp. 1)
козёл 'goat', ко́злик (dim.-hyp. 1), козлёнок (dim. 1), козлёночек (dim.-hyp. 3)
коро́ва 'cow', коро́вка (dim. 1), коро́вушка (hyp. 2), коровёнка (disp. 2)
ку́рица 'hen', ку́рочка (dim.-hyp. 1)
ло́шадь 'horse', лоша́дка (dim.-hyp. 1), лошадёнка (disp. 2), лоша́дочка dim.-hyp. 3)
лягу́шка 'frog', лягушо́нок (dim. 1), лягушо́ночек (hyp. 3)
му́ха 'fly', му́шка (dim. 1), му́шечка (dim.-hyp. 3)
мышь 'mouse', мы́шка (dim. 1), мышо́нок (dim. 1), мышо́ночек (hyp. 3)
обезья́на 'monkey', обезья́нка (dim.-hyp. 1), обезья́ночка (dim.-hyp. 3)
овца́ 'sheep', ове́чка (dim.-hyp. 1)
орёл 'eagle', орлёнок (dim.-hyp. 1), орлёночек (dim.-hyp. 3)
пету́х 'cock', петушо́к (dim.-hyp. 1), пе́тенька (hyp. 2)
ры́ба 'fish', ры́бка (dim.-hyp. 1), рыбёшка (disp. 2), ры́бонька (hyp. 2)
соба́ка 'dog', соба́чка (dim.-hyp. 1), собачо́нка (disp. 2), собачо́ночка (hyp. 3)
со́кол 'falcon', соко́лик (hyp. 1)
солове́й 'nightingale', соло́вушка (hyp. 2)
стрекоза́ 'dragon-fly', стреко́зочка (dim.-hyp. 3)
телёнок 'calf', телёночек (hyp. 3)
тигр 'tiger', тигрёнок (dim. 1), тигрёночек (dim.-hyp. 3)
у́тка 'duck', у́точка (dim.-hyp. 1), утёнок (dim. 1), утёночек (dim.-hyp. 3)
червя́к 'worm', червячо́к (dim. 1), червячи́шко (disp. 2)
чиж 'siskin', чи́жик (dim. 1), чижо́нок (dim. 1), чижо́ночек (dim.-hyp. 3)

Trees and plants

берёза 'birch', берёзка (dim.-hyp. 1), берёзонька (hyp. 2), берёзочка (dim.-hyp. 3)
гриб 'mushroom', грибо́к (dim.-hyp. 1), грибо́чек (dim.-hyp. 3)
дуб 'oak', дубо́к (dim. 1), дубо́чек (dim.-hyp. 3)
ель 'fir', ёлочка (dim.-hyp. 3)
и́ва 'willow', и́вушка (hyp. 2)
кали́на 'guelder rose', кали́нка (hyp. 1), кали́нушка (hyp. 2)
капу́ста 'cabbage', капу́стка (hyp. 1), капу́сточка (dim.-hyp. 3)
клён 'maple', кленóк (dim. 1), кленóчек (dim.-hyp. 3)
куст 'bush', ку́стик (dim. 1), кусто́чек (hyp. 3)

---

[1] Gen. pl. No other forms occur.

корень 'root', корешок (dim. 1), корешочек (dim.-hyp. 3)
лес 'wood', лесок (dim.-hyp. 1), лесочек (dim.-hyp. 3)
липа 'lime', липка (dim. 1), липочка (dim.-hyp. 3)
малина 'raspberry', малинка (hyp. 1), малиночка (hyp. 3)
орех 'nut', орешек (dim.-hyp. 1)
осина 'aspen', осинка (dim. 1), осиночка (dim.-hyp. 3)
пень 'stump', пенёк (dim. 1), пенёчек (dim.-hyp. 3)
помидор 'tomato', помидорчик (dim.-hyp. 1)
роза 'rose', розочка (dim.-hyp. 3)
роща 'coppice', рощица (dim.-hyp. 1)
рябина 'rowan', рябинка (dim. 1), рябиночка (dim.-hyp. 3), рябинушка (hyp. 2)
сад 'garden', садик (dim. 1), садок (dim.-hyp. 1), садочек (dim.-hyp. 3)
сорняк 'weed', сорнячок (fam. 1)
сосна 'pine', сосенка (hyp. 1), сосёнка (disp. 2), сосёночка (hyp. 3)
трава 'grass', травка (dim.-hyp. 1), травушка (hyp. 2)
цветок 'flower', цветочек (dim.-hyp. 1)
черешня 'bird-cherry', черешенка (dim.-hyp. 1)
черника 'bilberry', черничка (dim.-hyp. 1)
чеснок 'garlic', чесночок (dim.-hyp. 1)
яблоня 'apple-tree', яблонька (dim.-hyp. 1)

Natural phenomena
ветер 'wind', ветерок (dim.-hyp. 1), ветерочек (dim.-hyp. 3)
дождь 'rain', дождик (dim. 1), дождичек (dim.-hyp. 3)
заря 'dawn', зорька (dim.-hyp. 1), зорюшка (hyp. 2), зоренька (dim.-hyp. 2)
звезда 'star', звёздочка (dim.-hyp. 1)
земля 'earth', землица (hyp. 1), земелька (hyp. 1)
зима 'winter', зимушка (hyp. 2)
мороз 'frost', морозец (dim.-hyp. 1), морозишко (disp. 2)
облако 'cloud', облачко (dim.-hyp. 1)
огонь 'fire', огонёк (dim. 1), огонёчек (dim.-hyp. 3)
снег 'snow', снежок (dim.-hyp. 1), снежочек (dim.-hyp. 3)
солнце 'sun', солнышко (hyp. 2)
туча 'cloud', тучка (dim.-hyp. 1)

The house
балкон 'balcony', балкончик (dim.-hyp. 1)
дверь 'door', дверца (dim. 1)
дом 'house', домик (dim. 1), домок (dim. 1), домишко (disp. 2), домишечко (dim.-hyp. 3)
здание 'building', зданьице (dim. 1)
квартира 'flat', квартирка (dim. 1), квартирочка (dim.-hyp. 3)
ключ 'key', ключик (dim. 1)
комната 'room', комнатка (dim. 1), комнатушка (dim.-hyp. 2), комнатёнка (disp. 2), комнатушечка (dim.-hyp. 3)
кухня 'kitchen', кухонька (dim.-hyp. 2)
окно 'window', оконце (dim. 1), окошко (dim. 2), окошечко (dim.-hyp. 3)

помеще́ние 'lodging', помеще́ньице (disp. 1)
спа́льня 'bedroom', спа́ленка (dim.-hyp. 1)
ха́та 'hut', ха́тка (dim. 1), хатёнка (disp. 2), ха́точка (dim.-hyp. 3), хатёночка (hyp. 3)

Household objects

ба́нка 'tin', ба́ночка (dim. 1)
буты́лка 'bottle', буты́лочка (dim. 1)
ва́за 'vase', ва́зочка (dim. 3)
ви́лка 'fork', ви́лочка (dim.-hyp. 1)
графи́н 'carafe', графи́нчик (dim.-hyp. 1)
дива́н 'divan', дива́нчик (dim.-hyp. 1)
кастрю́ля 'saucepan', кастрю́лька (dim. 1)
кре́сло 'armchair', кре́слице (dim.-hyp. 1)
крова́ть 'bed', крова́тка (dim.-hyp. 1), крова́точка (dim.-hyp. 3)
кру́жка 'jug', кру́жечка (dim.-hyp. 1)
ло́жка 'spoon', ло́жечка (dim. 1)
нож 'knife', но́жик (dim. 1), но́жичек (dim.-hyp. 3)
одея́ло 'blanket', одея́льце (dim. 1)
простыня́ 'sheet', просты́нка (dim. 1)
салфе́тка 'napkin', салфе́точка (dim.-hyp. 1)
стака́н 'glass', стака́нчик (dim. 1)
стол 'table', сто́лик (dim. 1), столи́шко (disp. 2)
стул 'chair', сту́льчик (dim. 1)
таре́лка 'plate', таре́лочка (dim. 1)
ча́шка 'cup', ча́шечка (dim. 1)
шкаф 'cupboard', шка́фик and шка́фчик (dim. 1)

Materials

антраци́т 'anthracite', антраци́тик (hyp. 1)
асфа́льт 'asphalt', асфа́льтик (hyp. 1)
бума́га 'paper', бума́жка (dim. 1), бумажо́нка (disp. 2), бума́жечка (dim.-hyp. 3), бумажо́чка (hyp. 3)
вода́ 'water', води́ца (hyp. 1) води́чка (hyp. 3)
зо́лото 'gold', зо́лотце (hyp. 1), золоти́шко (disp. 2)
изумру́д 'emerald', изумру́дик (hyp. 1)
ка́мень 'stone', ка́мешек (dim.-hyp. 1)
кана́т 'rope', кана́тик (hyp. 1), кана́тишко (disp. 2)
кероси́н 'kerosine', кероси́нчик (hyp. 1)
кирпи́ч 'brick', кирпи́чик (hyp. 1), кирпичи́шко (disp. 2)
ма́рля 'gauze', ма́рлица (hyp. 1)
мел 'chalk', мело́к (hyp. 1)
песо́к 'sand', песо́чек (hyp. 3)
соло́ма 'straw', соло́мка (hyp. 1)
у́голь 'coal', уголёк (hyp. 1), уголёчек (dim.-hyp. 3)
флане́ль 'flannel', флане́лька (hyp. 1)

People, nationalities, professions

актёр 'actor', актёришка (disp. 2)
америка́нка 'American woman', америка́ночка (dim.-hyp. 1)

англича́нка 'Englishwoman', англича́ночка (dim.-hyp. 1)
аристокра́т 'aristocrat', аристокра́тик (disp. 1), аристокра́тишка (disp. 2)
арти́стка 'artiste', арти́сточка (cond. 1)
аспира́нт 'post-graduate', аспира́нтик (iron. 1)
ассисте́нт 'assistant', ассисте́нтик (iron. 1)
ба́ба 'peasant woman', бабёнка (disp. 2)
господи́н 'gentleman', господи́нчик (iron. 1)
друг 'friend', дружо́к (hyp. 1), дружо́чек (hyp. 3)
защи́тник 'defending counsel', защи́тничек (disp. 1)
земля́к 'fellow-countryman', землячо́к (hyp. 1)
идио́т 'idiot', идио́тик (cont. 2)
купе́ц 'merchant', купчи́шка (disp. 2)
ма́льчик 'boy', мальчо́нка (hyp. 2), мальчо́нок (hyp. 1), мальчи́шка (disp. 2), мальчо́ночек (hyp. 3), мальчи́шечка (hyp. 3)
матро́с 'sailor', матро́сик (dim.-hyp. 1), матро́сишка (disp. 2)
моря́к 'seaman', морячо́к (dim.-hyp. 1)
ня́ня 'nannie', ня́нька (disp. 1), ня́нюшка (hyp. 2), ня́нечка (hyp. 3)
па́рень 'lad', паренёк (dim.-hyp. 1), парни́шка (cond. 2), парни́шечка (hyp. 3)
пасту́х 'shepherd', пастушо́к (dim.-hyp. 1), пастушо́нок (dim.-hyp. 1), пастушо́ночек (hyp. 3)
по́вар 'cook', поварёнок (dim.-hyp. 1)
подру́га 'girl friend', подру́жка (dim.-hyp. 1), подру́жечка (dim.-hyp. 3), подру́женька (hyp. 2)
помо́щник 'assistant', помо́щничек (iron. 1)
рабо́тник 'worker', рабо́тничек (iron. 1)
стари́к 'old man', старичо́к (dim.-hyp. 1), старика́шка (disp. 2), старика́шечка (cond. 3)
стару́ха 'old woman', стару́шка (dim.-hyp. 1), старушо́нка (disp. 2), стару́шечка (hyp. 3)
собесе́дник 'collocutor', собесе́дничек (iron. 1)
солда́т 'soldier', солда́тик (dim.-hyp. 1), солда́тушка (hyp. 2)
студе́нт 'student', студе́нтик (dim.-hyp. 1), студе́нтишка (disp. 2)
те́нор 'tenor', теноро́к (disp. 1)
тип 'type', ти́пик (cont. 1)
хозя́ин 'master', хозя́йчик (disp. 1)
хозя́йка 'landlady, housewife', хозя́юшка (hyp. 2)
царь 'tsar', царёк (iron. 1)
чуда́к 'eccentric, crank', чудачо́к (dim.-hyp. 1)

Time

ве́чер 'evening', вечеро́к (hyp. 1), вечеро́чек (hyp. 3)
воскресе́нье 'Sunday', воскресе́ньице (iron. 1)
вто́рник 'Tuesday', вто́рничек (iron. 1)
год 'year', го́дик (hyp. 1), годо́к (hyp. 1), годо́чек (hyp. 3)
день 'day', денёк (hyp. 1), денёчек (hyp. 3)
зима́ 'winter', зи́мушка (hyp. 2)
ме́сяц 'month', ме́сячишко (disp. 2)
мину́та 'minute', мину́тка (dim.-hyp. 1), мину́точка (hyp. 3)
ночь 'night', но́чка (hyp. 1), но́ченька (hyp. 2)

полчаса́ 'half an hour', полча́сика (dim.-hyp. 1)
понеде́льник 'Monday', понеде́льничек (iron. 1)
сезо́н 'season', сезо́нчик (iron. 2)
секу́нда 'second', секу́ндочка (dim.-hyp. 1)
суббо́та 'Saturday', суббо́тка (fam. 1)
у́тро 'morning', у́течко (ingrat. 1)

Measures

килогра́мм 'kilogramme', килогра́ммчик (dim.-hyp. 1)
пята́к 'five-copeck piece', пятачо́к (hyp. 1)
пятёрка 'five', пятёрочка (hyp. 1)
тро́йка 'three, troika' тро́ечка (hyp. 1)
ты́сяча 'thousand', тысчо́нка (disp. 2), тысчо́ночка (fam., hyp. 3)
четвёрка 'four', четвёрочка (hyp. 1)
че́тверть 'quarter', четерти́нка (dim.-hyp. 1), четверту́шка (hyp. 2), четверти́ночка (hyp. 3)
шту́ка 'piece', шту́чка (hyp. 1)

Abstract nouns

быт 'way of life', бы́тик (iron. 1)
во́ля 'will', во́люшка (hyp. 2)
весть 'news', ве́сточка (hyp. 3)
го́ре 'grief', го́рюшко[1] (dim., comp. 2)
ду́ма 'thought', ду́мушка[1] (hyp. 2)
заблужде́нье 'error', заблужде́ньице (ingrat. 1)
забо́та 'care', забо́тушка (hyp. 2)
здоро́вье 'health', здоро́вьице (ingrat. 1), здоро́вьишко (disp. 2)
иде́я 'idea', иде́йка (disp. 1)
иди́ллия 'idyll', иди́ллийка (iron. 1)
мировоззре́ние 'view of the world, Weltanschauung', мировоззре́ньице (iron. 1)
пра́вда 'truth', пра́вдочка (iron. 1)
рабо́та 'work', рабо́тка (iron. 1), работёнка (disp. 2), работёночка (hyp. 3)
си́ла 'strength', си́лушка (hyp. 2)
смерть 'death', сме́ртушка (hyp. 3)
тео́рия 'theory', тео́рийка (iron. 1)
ую́т 'comfort', ую́тик (iron. 1)
хо́лод 'cold', холодо́к (dim.-hyp. 1)
хрипота́ 'hoarseness', хрипотца́ (dim. 1)
ю́мор 'humour', юморо́к (fam. hyp. 1)

BIBLIOGRAPHY

BELIĆ, A. 'Zur Entwicklungsgeschichte der slavischen Diminutiv- und Amplicativ-Suffixes', *Archiv für Slavische Philologie*. Leipzig, 1901, XXIII, 137–206.
BELIĆ, A. 'Природа и происхождение существительных субъективной оценки', *IУ международный съезд славистов: материалы, дис-*

---

[1] The use of diminutive forms in -ушка/-юшка and -юшко from abstract nouns is typical of folk literature (*byliny*, songs, dirges).

куссии, т. 2, — *Проблемы славянского языкознания.* Академия наук, Moscow, 1958, 180–81.

BULLOCH, J. M. 'Some Scottish Characteristics—The Delight of the Doric in the Diminutive', *The Scottish Tongue, A series of lectures delivered to...the Burns Club* (W. A. Craigie *et al.*), London, 1924.

CHERNYSHOV, V. I. 'Русские уменьшительно-ласкательные личные имена', *Русский язык в школе.* Moscow, 1947, no. 4.

DEMENT'YEV, A. 'Уменьшительные слова в русском языке', *Русский язык в школе.* Moscow, 1953, no. 5.

DIETH, E. *A Grammar of the Buchan Dialect.* Cambridge, 1932.

FERRELL, J. 'The second locative case (in -*ú*) from diminutive nouns formed by means of the morpheme -#*k*- in contemporary literary Russian', *For Roman Jakobson; essays on the occasion of his sixtieth birthday...*, M. Halle *et al.* (Eds.). Mouton, The Hague, 1956.

GALKINA-FEDORUK, YE. M. 'Об экспрессивности и эмоциональности в языке', *Сборник статей по языкознанию посвященный профессору Московского университета Академику В. В. Виноградову* (ed. A. I. Yefimov). МГУ, Moscow, 1958.

GALKINA-FEDORUK, YE. M. *et al. Современный русский язык, ч. 2.* Moscow, 1964.

IVANOV, V. 'Тохарская параллель к славянским уменьшительным формам', *IУ международный съезд славистов: материалы, дискуссии, т. 2 — Проблемы славянского языкознания.* Академия наук, Moscow, 1958, 82.

IVANOVA, N. F. 'Наречия с суффиксом эмоциональной оценки -еньк- (-оньк-) в современном русском языке', *Русский язык в школе.* Moscow, 1965, no. 1.

JESPERSEN, O. *A Modern English Grammar.* London, 1954, vol. VI.

LAPTEVA, O. D. 'Личные собствсенные имена с суффиксами субъективной оценки в современном русском языке', *Учёные записки МГПИ им. В. И. Ленина.* Moscow, 1958, vol. CXXII.

MANDEL'SHTAM, I. E. 'Об уменьшительных суффиксах в русском языке со стороны их значения', *Журнал министерства народного просвещения.* St Petersburg, 1903, nos. 7, 8, 9.

OGOL'TSOV, V. M. 'Эмоциональные и экспрессивные значения суффикса имен прилагательных -еньк- (-оньк-)', *Русский язык в школе.* Moscow, 1960, no. 2.

OGOL'TSOV, V. M. 'Об источниках экспрессивности (выразительности) форм субъективной оценки качества имен прилагательных', *Филологический сборник.* Alma-Ata, 1963.

PLYAMOVATAYA, S. S. 'О грамматической природе и классификации имен существительных с уменьшительно-экспрессивными суффиксами в современном русском языке', *Русский язык в школе.* Moscow, 1955, no. 6.

PLYAMOVATAYA, S. S. *Размерно-оценочные имена существительные в современном русском языке.* Moscow, 1961.

ROTZOLL, E. 'Die Deminutivbildungen im Neuenglischen, unter besonderer Berücksichtigung der Dialekte', *Anglistische Forschungen.* Heidelberg, 1910, vol. 31.

RUKE-DRAVINA, V. *Diminutive im Lettischen.* London, 1959.

SHMELYOV, D. N. 'Об одном случае активной аналогии в современном русском языке (существительное с суффиксом -инка)', *Развитие современного русского языка* (S. Ozhegov and M. Panov, eds.). Moscow, 1963.

UNBEGAUN, B. O. *Russian Grammar*. O.U.P., Oxford, 1960.

VINOGRADOV, V. V. *Русский язык (грамматическое учение о слове)*. Учпедгиз, Moscow–Leningrad, 1947.

VINOGRADOV, V. V. *et al. Грамматика русского языка*. Академия наук, Moscow, 1966, vol. 1.

WARD, D. *The Russian Language Today*. Hutchinson, London, 1965.

ZANDVOORT, R. W. *A Handbook of English Grammar*. Groningen, 1950.